Song of Triumph

Song of Triumph

Eleanor Veldman Grotenhuis

BAKER BOOK HOUSE
Grand Rapids, Michigan 49516

Copyright 1991 by
Baker Book House Company

ISBN: 0-8010-3845-6

Second printing, April 1992

Printed in the United States of America

To Dale

his selfless love and encouragement
his honesty and objectivity
his good judgment
his unshakeable confidence in me
provided the necessary impetus to
see Jack's story to the finish line.

Together we suffered
together we enjoy the privilege of seeing
Jack's life, death, and enduring testimony in print.

Great and marvelous are your deeds,
Lord God Almighty!

With gratitude to God for

Jack Michael Grotenhuis

January 5, 1956—December 8, 1983

Contents

Foreword

A comforter, says the Bible, is someone who stands beside us to help, a person who takes some of our pain and gives us some of his or her strength. Eleanor Grotenhuis is a comforter. She knows the terrain of the valley of sorrow. We walk it with her and her husband Dale as she tells their story.

People wounded by death and sorrow journey back to life by facing their grief. This story is realistic. It provides no easy answers or explanations, but it elicits many questions and expresses honest emotions. You will feel the pain, taste the tears, ask the questions that have no answers, and discover the strength to live again.

Even when we know death is coming, none of us is ready for its arrival. No one tells us how physical grief is, how our bodies ache. Grief is illogical and irrational; no matter how hard we try, it doesn't make sense. It seems as if life should stop. But it keeps going, and so must we.

Comfort comes from many sources. We find it with the friend who lets us cry and just listens when we talk. It takes us through the promises of God and into prayer. Knowing we're not the only ones who ever felt the way we feel or thought what we think comforts us. Finding that others have walked the path of sorrow and survived reassures us. The greatest comfort is becoming a comforter to someone else.

It is a paradox that an anthem of praise can be born from agony of soul. But that is God's way: from his death on the cross, Jesus brought life everlasting. *Song of Triumph* testifies to God's ability to bring strength out of our weakness. Here is a story that communicates the ministry of comfort. May God use it to bring healing to broken hearts.

David Wiersbe
Roscoe, Illinois

Preface

"The spirit indeed is willing, but the flesh is weak" (Matt. 26:41).

My flesh is protesting the writing of this book. Why deliberately open deep wounds that are beginning to heal? Why relive painful memories?

The Spirit compels me to share some of the personal experiences through which God brought me and my family. I want to honor our heavenly Father throughout these pages. He did not leave our souls in the pit of hopelessness but dramatically displayed the magnitude of his daily mercies, love, and faithfulness.

I wish to pay tribute to our beloved son Jack, who gave us twenty-seven years of great joy. I do not seek pity, nor do I wish to place Jack on a pedestal. I do remember that he lived and made a contribution to the church, education, society, and to his family and host of friends.

Grief is abominably lonely. I have adopted my typewriter as my therapeutic friend. I will put my innermost thoughts on paper as a legacy to my children and grandchildren.

Finally, I want to give encouragement and renewed hope to families who are mourning the death of a loved one. This book is also for those who fearfully ask, "How can people like *us* help people like *you?*" I pray that these pages will give the reader a better understanding of the mind and heart of the griever.

Part One

Great and marvelous are your deeds, Lord God Almighty

1

Preparation

"ONCE upon a time" is a good way to begin, because we the Grotenhuis family lived such a fairy-tale existence. We truly "lived happily." Good health, extensive family travels, and exciting professional experiences characterized our lives. The name *Grotenhuis* means "great house," and appropriately we lived in a large attractive house on a big corner lot. Most important, Jesus Christ was head of our household.

Dale, the father and my husband, was recognized as a published composer. Since 1959 he had been professor of music and chairman of choral activities at Dordt College in Sioux Center, Iowa (a small, Christian, liberal arts college). I, Eleanor Veldman Grotenhuis, was a homemaker, former teacher, and professional speaker. Together we had four sons. Jack, age twenty-seven, was completing doctoral studies in music at Arizona State University in Tempe. Bob, age twenty-five, was a television news anchor in Sioux City, Iowa. Phil, age twenty-one, was a senior at Dordt College. Tom, age ten, was in fourth grade at Sioux Center Christian School.

Life for us was comfortable, pleasant, and very tidy. I felt this fairy-tale existence could not last forever and had expressed the thought to my only sister, Laurie. I told her, "One of these days we are going to lose either Mother or Dad, and life is going to change." We counted our blessings and our years free of major setbacks. Laurie and I agreed that, while a person would not deliberately pray for adversity, "In the world you have tribulation" (John 16:33). We should prepare for it while times are good.

Preparation lies in the diligent study of God's Word, a vigorous prayer life, seeking the fellowship of God's people, and living in gratitude. Just as a farmer prepares for the cold, barren winter by filling his silo with food for his hungry livestock, so the Christian gets ready for the winter of sorrow by filling his spiritual silo, his soul, with spiritual food.

Laurie and I determined to lead more faithful devotional lives.

"Prepare to meet your God" (Amos 4:12).

2

Golden Bubble

DECEMBER 6, 1983, began as a day to "rejoice and be glad." It was Tuesday. Just as hot pink is my favorite color and ten is my favorite number, so Tuesday is my favorite day. (Sounds like Sesame Street!) With a light heart I planned my day's activities. I would bake my outrageously expensive and high-calorie Christmas candied fruitcake, not the kind with citron or lemon peel but with lots of nuts and candied fruit. I rationalized that Christmas comes but once a year, and the recipe served many who would enjoy it—especially me! The fact that I was the local leader of a major weight-loss organization pricked my conscience. I eased the guilt by planning a low-calorie fish dinner for our evening meal. I would spend most of my day addressing Christmas cards, adding warm-fuzzy notes to family and friends. I was mentally set for a productive and enjoyable day.

The gently falling snow magnified my festive and nostalgic mood. There was much to anticipate. The Christmas season in the Dordt College music department is exciting. My role as a director's wife is rich and blessed.

My thoughts turned to Christmas vacation and our anticipated reunion in Arizona with son Jack and his wife, Kathy. Little brother Tom was especially eager, because he was going to explore Squaw Peak with Jack and eat at McDonald's when they completed their climb.

Life always seemed an adventure when we watched son Bob anchor the six and ten o'clock news on television. I reflected on my godly parents, their good health, my sister and brothers, their spouses and children, and our combined blessings. Psalm 16:6 (NIV) came to my mind: "The boundary lines have fallen for me in pleasant places."

All of my senses seemed finely tuned to the joy of the season: the sound of beautiful music on the stereo, the aroma of the irresistible fruitcake wafting from the oven, the sight of a spacious home surrounded by fresh-fallen snow. I felt overwhelming gratitude to God, the giver of these gifts. I savored every moment of my life. Truly, I was unacquainted with grief.

I sat down with a mug of coffee and began to write my Christmas cards. To a high school friend I expressed, "Life is like a golden bubble; one wonders when it will burst. . . ."

"I will sing to the LORD, because he has dealt bountifully with me" (Ps. 13:6).

3

Faith on Trial

I did not finish that sentence, because I was interrupted by the sound of the telephone. At that moment, 3:30 P.M., December 6, 1983, my golden bubble burst—permanently.

The voice at the other end was gentle. "Are you the mother of Jack Grotenhuis?" he asked. "This is the Arizona State Police Department. Ma'am, I would like you to sit down, because I'm afraid that I have bad news for you."

My mind began to play tricks on me as I refused to comprehend the implications of this call. Did Jack lose his driver's license? Was he caught for speeding? Was he robbed? The thought of an accident never entered my mind. What marvelous defense mechanisms our gracious God provides, enabling us to keep functioning in hideous moments.

Slowly I absorbed the information as words began to register one by one: "motorcycle accident . . . helicopter . . . in a coma . . . intensive care . . . severe bleeding in the brain . . . call the hospital immediately." I alternately became hot, cold, faint, nauseous.

The accident report told the details: At 11:30 A.M., Jack was headed for Arizona State University, driving his motorcycle. The driver of the car stated: "I was stopped at Geneva and Mill Streets, waiting to turn left. I looked to the left, then to the right for passing cars. It looked clear, so I started to make my left turn. Then I saw him. A motorist on a motorcycle from the left. It was hard to see him because of the sun shining. He ran into the left

20

side of my car." Jack became airborne and struck the windshield of an oncoming car. His only injuries were a punctured lung and severely injured brain. His helmet saved him from more cuts and bruises.

There was a complication. The only identification in Jack's billfold was his student ID card from Dordt College, and only by calling the college did the police department locate us, his parents. They were not aware initially that Jack was married; a couple of hours later they finally notified his wife, Kathy.

Meanwhile, it had been a curious day for Kathy. She had not felt well, having been overcome with a sense of malaise the moment she awakened. At 11:30 A.M., the exact time of Jack's accident, she became ill and faint. She stopped working, rested in the lounge of the bank where she was the assistant manager, and rued the fact that she had not followed Jack's urging that morning to stay home and "sleep it off."

I shook uncontrollably as I dialed the number of the hospital in Phoenix. The prognosis was not encouraging; Jack was in a deep coma.

"Is he going to die?" I fearfully inquired.

"I don't know," the doctor cautiously replied, "but there is severe bleeding in the brain, and I would advise you to fly here as soon as possible." He asked if I was going to be all right, and shakily I responded that we were Christians. He assured me that our faith would get us through this trauma.

I felt the presence of the Holy Spirit groaning in my behalf.

Strange as it may seem, I was overcome by two distinct sensations. One was that of Satan, gleefully taunting me: "*This* is the work of your loving God?" I knew that all of my beliefs, taught in my Christian home, church, and school, were going to be put to the supreme test. Part with Jack? No, no! Never! My faith was on trial from that moment on.

21

Secondly, I had a mental picture of Jack. He was sitting in a wheelchair, staring at me with dull, uncomprehending eyes, instead of those warm brown eyes I loved. With the receiver still in my trembling hands, I dropped to my knees and prayed, "God, I have two requests. Please, dear Lord, take Jack to yourself, and please keep me from the power of the evil one." I considered that heaven would be great gain for him; he was ready.

I never prayed to keep his life at any cost.

"Prove me, O LORD, and try me; test my heart and my mind" (Ps. 26:2).

4

Automatic Pilot

ONE moment we were relishing life with all of its joys, and the next moment we were stumbling "through the valley of the shadow of death." Without warning, life as we had known it ceased to exist. Dale, suddenly called out of the Dordt College choir's rehearsal, walked through our front door with a face as white as the new snow in the front yard. We wordlessly hugged, feeling weak and helpless to comfort each other.

Then in the most remarkable way, God with his unlimited power put us on "automatic pilot," enabling us to deal with the business at hand. We both knew we had miles to go before we slept. The house filled with people who came and went and helped us make decisions. We made the necessary telephone calls, leaving a trail of stunned and saddened relatives.

Robotlike, I did the dishes, put away the defrosted fish, and wrapped and froze the candied fruitcake. How unappetizing it all looked! The Christmas decorations, which an hour before had been beautifully eye catching, now struck me as offensive and ugly. I willed my brain, my legs, my hands to keep moving, pleading with God to help me. I wanted to scream, to flail my arms, to explode. I wanted to die. I could not face the loss of one of our magnificent boys.

By 10:30 P.M., the preparations for our flight to Phoenix were complete. Our suitcases were packed, plane tickets purchased, and hair shampooed and set. We had devotions with our close friends, just the four of us. With heavy hearts and stunned brains we listened to

23

the words of Psalm 34:18 NIV: "The LORD is close to the brokenhearted." For the first time in our lives we knew what brokenhearted meant. It is actual physical pain. It is a ripping apart of one's insides, leaving only the shell intact. We were engulfed in a feeling of complete helplessness. We were consumed with fear, anxiety, despair.

We kissed our friends goodbye, grateful for their comfort, for God's presence, and each other. We slept fitfully. We could scarcely bear the thought of Jack, lying unconscious, 1700 miles distant. Would he survive this night?

"When you pass through the waters I will be with you; and through the rivers, they shall not overwhelm you" (Isa. 43:2).

5

Birth Trauma

JACK MICHAEL GROTENHUIS entered and departed this life with trauma. His was a long, forty-eight hour delivery, with serious complications, culminating at 12:30 P.M. on January 5, 1956. The delivery room in St. Joseph's Hospital, Bellingham, Washington, faced the Bellingham Bay, which was unusually stormy. I recall saying to the attending nurse, "The wind is howling, and so am I."

The doctor's words to my distraught husband were not encouraging. The prolonged labor was due to a structural deformity in the pelvis, making delivery almost impossible. Time was of the essence, and the doctor was hampered by circumstances; a gynecologist's convention in Seattle took every obstetric specialist in the city. In desperation he sought the help of a kidney specialist. "Be prepared to lose your wife, or your child, or both," he warned Dale. And he added, "If your child lives, he will likely be mentally impaired."

By God's grace, though bruised from delivery and yellow with jaundice, Jack survived the odds. In fact, he proved to be exceptionally bright and unusually gifted. And I, his mother, through that brush-with-death experience, was ushered into mature womanhood.

"Be prepared to lose your child!" Just how does one prepare for a personal catastrophe of such magnitude? Had we known how brief his life would be, would we have lived differently? I doubt it. We made many mistakes, but we never claimed to be infallible parents. We are weak and sinful human beings and only did what each time seemed wisest and best. It is a comfort that

God forgives *all* of our sins and shortcomings, as individuals and as parents. We leave our "if onlies" with him.

Jack, my son! I screamed when he entered this world, I wailed when he departed. Gladly would I have gone in his place. Never could I have imagined such bone-crushing agony. Yet, I thank God for the joy he gave us in those brief twenty-seven years. And with Alfred Lord Tennyson, I declare with all my heart: I would rather have loved him and lost him than never to have loved him at all.

"Fear not, for I have redeemed you; I have called you by name, you are mine" (Isa. 43:1).

6

Last Look

I last saw Jack vigorously alive in May 1983. We decided to celebrate the end of another enjoyable year of teaching at Dordt College by flying to Phoenix and spending a few days with Jack and Kathy. In spite of temperatures reaching 116 degrees, we had grand fellowship. We enthusiastically made plans for Christmastime when we would be together again as a family in Arizona. What fun it would be to see the Grand Canyon, to go over the border into Mexico, to leave the cold of an Iowa winter for the warmth of the southwest! We joyed in anticipation as we kissed goodbye at the Phoenix airport. Strangely, while my husband confirmed our plane reservations, I felt compelled to run after Jack. As he quickly departed for the parking lot, I strained for a last glimpse of him. I cried, not because I was sad, but because I loved him so much. Had I known that I would never again see his always hurried, purposeful stride, I would have caught up with him and blurted, "I forgot to say that I love you."

"You do not know about tomorrow. What is your life? For you are a mist that appears for a little time and then vanishes" (James 4:14).

7

Composer in the Audience

I vividly recall our conversation of November 10, 1983 as we drank coffee together in the den. I was encouraging Dale to make a quick trip to Phoenix. "Next week is Jack's doctoral conducting recital, and you belong there. After all, how many fathers have sons who are cut so completely out of the same cloth as you two are? Life can be very short. *How do we know how long we will have him?* I hope you go!"

With zest we packed two suitcases for this very special weekend trip. One of them was filled with gaily-wrapped Christmas presents for the entire family, to be opened in a little over a month. Along with these tangible gifts God enclosed his intangible, priceless love offering: a most beautiful, final, memorable musical experience for my husband and son. On November 20, Jack conducted the Arizona State Graduate School Chorale with musicianship and finesse, ending the concert with "Blessed Be the Name of the Lord." The video tape shows Jack turning around to the audience and announcing, "I am privileged to have the composer of this closing anthem in the audience; in fact, he is my father, and I am so happy he is here." His dad acknowledged the applause and the broad smiles on the faces of Jack's graduate school friends. Little did this choir realize that within two weeks they would be sitting with Jack's parents in the intensive care unit of a hospital and then singing once more at Jack's memorial service in the Palm Lane Christian Reformed Church in Phoenix.

It had been a gratifying weekend for father and son, and conversation was animated as they ate breakfast together in the airport restaurant. They discussed their many mutual interests, Jack's recital, his dissertation, his coming interview in January for a teaching position in the Dordt College music department. Summing it up, Jack said, "Dad, I'm almost finished with the degree, and now all I want to do is serve the Lord."

Then came the final boarding call at the departure gate, quick hugs, enduring words. "Jack, I love you, and I am so proud of you!"

It had been an exquisite relationship from start to finish.

"I shall go to him, but he will not return to me" (2 Sam. 12:23).

Part Two

Just and true are your ways, King of the ages

Lord, _____ Just and true _ are all your ways; You, O

Lord God Al - might - y, Just and true _ are all your ways; You, O

Lord, _____ Just and true _ are all your ways; You, O

Lord God Al - might - y, Just and true _ are all your ways; You, O

8

Communion of the Saints

OUR hearts were heavy as we drove through cold predawn hours to Eppley Airfield in Omaha, Nebraska. We had a quiet resignation and an intuitive certainty that we were about to say a permanent good-bye to our eldest son. The police officer in Arizona and the neurologist were honest in telling us the medical prognosis. The telephone did not conceal their feelings of hopelessness. They did not allow us to fly to Phoenix with unrealistic expectations, which I respect and appreciate.

Along the winding road of grief, God used many people to prepare, support, encourage, and sustain us. I am reminded of the cleaning lady in the air terminal's rest room who heard my muffled sobs and asked, "Honey, what is the matter?" When I shared my pain with her, she responded, "I have a son who was in a motorcycle accident, too; he lived and he's not the same boy. Oh, honey, pray that he dies. Pray that he dies!" Two strangers with a common grief, we embraced and wept together.

Dale and I flew out of Omaha at 10:00 A.M., crying, praying. The sun streamed through the plane's window, and I recalled having read a devotional based on "Jehovah is my Sun and Shield." I felt God's warmth on my face and grasped these words: "I have loved you with an everlasting love" (Jer. 31:3 RSV). I saw the blue sky around and the cloud layer underneath us, and I believed that the plane was flying not on jet power but on prayer power. We were, from the very beginning, given a superhuman strength that defies description. We felt the reality of God's abundant grace and the effectiveness of the prayers of his people.

The dreaded moment came. We arrived at the Phoenix airport and were met by Jack's pastor. One look at his face told me that Jack would not recover. His condition had deteriorated during the night. As we drove to the hospital, I was keenly aware of the warm weather, the palm trees, the mountains, but had no aesthetic response. Beauty? Is anything beautiful? my mind cried out. Please, somebody! Tell me that this is all a bad dream. Oh God, help us. We can't spare Jack!

With apprehension we entered St. Joseph's Hospital and Trauma Center. We stepped out of the elevator, and Kathy ran toward us with arms outstretched. She was only twenty-three years old, stricken, fragile, like a bird with its wings clipped. The three of us clung to each other.

In the waiting room of the intensive care unit was a heart-warming gathering: the pastor and members of the First Christian Reformed Church, where Jack and Kathy were members; of the Palm Lane Christian Reformed Church, where Kathy directed the choir; of the Second Baptist Church, where Jack was the choir director. There were several Dordt College alumni, our surrogate children, and Arizona State University students and professors. We became like one big family with a tie that bound us—love for Jack. The words of our churches' creed, "I believe in the communion of saints," took on new meaning as we "waited on the Lord."

"Behold, how good and pleasant it is when brothers dwell in unity!" (Ps. 133:1).

9

Internal Injuries

THE nurse met us at the door of Jack's room. "Please talk to him," she said. "Even though he is unconscious, he can still hear." I don't know how true that was, but I do know that it was good therapy for me.

No dictionary contains the words to describe what parents feel when they see their child on a life-support system. Our protective instincts are useless. Complete helplessness paralyzes us. What a price all humankind has paid for sin—death! Our only hope lies in the unlimited power of God and who he is. Our only comfort is "that we belong, body and soul, to our Lord and Savior, Jesus Christ, who has fully satisfied for all our sins" (Heidelberg Catechism). Only in that light could I bend over Jack and whisper, "Today you are going to paradise!" And "I love you, Jack. Thank you for being such a wonderful son and soul buddy."

Tears flowed like a river from that room. I watched a heartbroken dad give up "the apple of his eye," his legacy to this earthly kingdom, the son who inherited his musical gifts, his priceless treasure, his beloved friend. Laying his head on Jack's motionless chest, Dale cried pitifully, "Jack, would that I could go in your place!"

At times it was difficult to believe that Jack was so severely injured. His injuries were virtually all internal. He was tan from the Arizona sun. He was lean and looked vigorous and healthy. However, the pressure on his brain continued to mount. The doctor kept us informed of the extent of the massive brain damage and finally called a family consultation to discuss organ donation. The decision was not difficult, as Jack had indicated in a recent letter his positive feelings about organ donation. He was considered the ideal donor because of his age, health, and the nature of his injuries.

We struggled, each of us in different ways. Jack had a teaching assistantship to the choral director of Arizona State University. Dr. McEwen and Jack enjoyed an enviable personal and working relationship based on mutual respect. This man expressed aloud what we all felt. Standing straight and tall, and speaking to no one in particular, he angrily declared, "I find this totally incomprehensible!"

Clasping my hand tightly, his wife whispered to me, "Jack was like our son, you know."

Kathy and Dale took a walk outside while I stayed with Jack. They met a gang of toughs, frittering away their time on a street corner near the hospital. The sight of them caused my normally kind husband to become uncharacteristically judgmental and enraged. With clenched fists, he furiously remarked to Kathy, "Tell me, what is going to be *their* contribution to this world? And there lies Jack, who only wants to serve the Lord with all his heart!"

"Behold, he snatches away; who can hinder him?
Who will say to him, 'What doest thou?'" (Job 9:12).

10

Why?

ALONE with Jack in that hospital room I, too, wrestled with the will of God. I asked questions that, humanly speaking, could not and still cannot be answered. I tenderly took his warm, limp hand in mine, studied his fingers and agonized. "God, do you mean to tell me that these sensitive fingers will never again play the piano? or the flute? or the oboe? And his rich baritone voice will forever be stilled? Why, then, did you lavish on him these musical gifts? And the generous scholarships—for what purpose?"

I put my face close to his and memorized every feature. I contemplated the knowledge and insights inside his head, the years of study, the diligent practice—to what avail? He was in a deep coma. The attending nurse had gently prepared us for the inevitable. "He can no longer walk or talk. He cannot comprehend," she had explained.

"God," I argued, "do you really know best? You instilled within this boy a yearning to use his abilities for your glory. You gave him the desire to serve you by inspiring others. Now you are depriving Jack of this privilege in an age dominated by 'what's-in-it-for-me.' Isn't this a mistake? Why? Is it because of something *I* have done? Are you punishing me?"

I was reminded of Moses, who was allowed to view the Promised Land, but was not permitted to enter it. Jack, too, had a glimpse of his Promised Land. In January, he was scheduled for an interview with the Dordt College board for a teaching position in the music department. He would graduate in May with his doctorate. In September he would possibly be teaching with his father at Dordt College, a fulfillment of his lifelong dream. Someday he even could take his father's place as chairman of choral activities. A member of the school administration later bemoaned, "We were pinning our hopes on Jack." It did not occur to any of us that God would interrupt such a logical, natural course of events. "'For my thoughts are not your thoughts, neither are your ways my ways,' declares the LORD" (Isa. 55:8 NIV).

Faith—"the assurance of things hoped for, the conviction of things not seen," (Heb. 11:1) was on trial. I felt weak and vulnerable.

"I believe; help my unbelief!" (Mark 9:24).

11

"I Mean It"

Jack's last brain scan was done shortly after noon, December 8. A team of medical experts shared the results with us. The monitor showed that all activity had ceased. Jack was brain-dead. It was obvious. His body seemed to droop, and the "light" had gone out of his eyes. His pupils were completely dilated. Jack had crossed the threshhold into the very presence of his heavenly Father!

Together we thanked God that, in his mercy, he did not allow Jack to live in a vegetative, unproductive state. The longer we live, the greater is our gratitude for that. Our hearts bleed when we meet head-trauma victims and their families.

The organ transplant medical team arrived to prepare Jack's body for surgery and the removal of his vital organs. Time was of the essence. Though I was sure of the decision, I found it most difficult to give up his eyes. Those warm brown eyes reflected his beautiful soul. I lagged behind, staying close to Jack. With my blurred vision I could see the doctors patiently waiting for me to let go. Suddenly, to my amazement, I heard a high-pitched, strained voice blurt out, "Wait a minute! 'The Lord gave and the Lord took away; blessed be the name of the Lord.' And I mean it!" It was my voice, but the Spirit within me was enabling me to give him up.

Had it been only *two* days before that I received the police officer's call about Jack's accident, and on my knees had begged of the Lord, "Please take Jack, and keep me from the power of the evil one"?

"Precious in the sight of the LORD is the death of his saints" (Ps. 116:15).

12

Gift of Life

WHAT a forlorn sight we were as we returned to the waiting room to await the completion of Jack's surgery. We felt deep anguish, abominable grief, and strangely, a sense of relief whenever we contemplated the alternative—Jack's living with massive brain damage. Yet, if need be, God gives grace to carry that burden, too, as many families of head-trauma survivors will testify.

The presence of Laurie and Ellis Deters, my sister and brother-in-law, sustained us. We felt deep gratitude for the Christ-like compassion, love, and ministry from the pastors and congregations in Phoenix as well. Unforgettable!

It was late afternoon when the surgeon appeared. His words were memorable. "The surgery is complete," he related. "We took the liver, pancreas, eyes, bone marrow, spleen, and the kidneys. You will be happy to know that we have found two perfect matches for his kidneys. One of the recipients is at this moment being flown by helicopter to the transplant center."

That moment is still vivid to me. I was exhilarated! I wanted to dance for joy! How pleased Jack would be to know that two people were about to receive a gift of life from him, the donor. And what a glorious Christmas gift for the recipients! Our loss was their gain. For a few precious moments we could lay our sorrow aside.

At that time we could not have envisioned that someday we would personally meet one of those "perfect matches." How often we underestimate the unlimited power of God to "do more abundantly than we could ask or think!" And because of our blessings in being part of

Jack's gift of life to others, I have since that day been making public speeches for the cause of organ donation.

> "For everything there is a season, and a time for every matter under heaven: a time to weep, and a time to laugh; a time to mourn, and a time to dance" (Eccles. 3:1, 4).

13

A Lesson in Priorities

WE left St. Joseph's Hospital and re-entered the outside world. But now we were marching to the beat of a different drummer, viewing everything and everyone through the eyes of the bereaved.

Physically I felt at the end of my rope; my knees kept buckling. I was mindful of a blazing, Arizona sunset and inwardly groaned, "Day is dying in the west, Lord, and so am I." We stopped at a restaurant for a late supper, where the dining room was decorated with a Christmas tree and tinsel. How distasteful it seemed! People were laughing at an adjoining table, and I couldn't tolerate the sound. I was convinced that we would never laugh again—never! I tried to pray before our meal, but the only words I could formulate were "God help us!" God seemed so far away!

We turned the key in the door to Kathy's apartment—now hers alone—and it literally screamed of Jack. His "presence" was everywhere. The Bible was where he had left it—in the middle of the kitchen table—well worn and used. Thank God! His creative talent stared us in the face. On the piano were four hymns that he had within the last week composed for the new *Psalter Hymnal* of the Christian Reformed Church. He had felt that the best of the lot was a setting of Psalm 17 (now included in the hymnal). Jack was looking forward to showing it to his dad at Christmastime, and over the last two measures he had written: "Eat your heart out, Dad." He was quite sure that his composer-father would wish he'd had those ideas first.

41

His neat, thick-volumed dissertation was in his study. We felt we were being stabbed. Of what use was that lengthy treatise? At that moment it seeemed to have been a waste of time and effort.

The Bible on the table, the music on the piano, the dissertation on the desk reminded us of an anonymous verse:

> We've only one life;
> 'Twill soon be past.
> And only what's done
> For *Christ* will last.

We learned a lesson in priorities that day.

"Seek first his kingdom and his righteousness" (Matt. 6:33 NIV).

14

Fighting for Survival

"MAN proposes, but God disposes." I pondered that adage the next day as I sadly repacked the empty suitcase with the Christmas gifts that had been brought to Phoenix so recently. The Bible tells us that when we make our plans, we should always add, ". . . if the Lord wills." I must always remember that.

Jack's body was being prepared for the flight to Iowa. It was Kathy's wish that he be buried in his home town. We spent much of the day planning both the memorial service in Phoenix that Friday evening and the funeral service in Sioux Center the following Tuesday.

We struggled through that day in the Slough of Despond. Only God's grace kept us functioning. Dale quietly left the apartment and revisited the scene of the accident, knocking on several doors and asking questions. Witnesses verified that Jack was unconscious immediately; there were no last words.

With aching hearts Kathy and I chose Jack's burial clothes. Dale brought the trash to the apartment complex dumpster; included was the badly torn jacket Jack had been wearing the morning of the accident. I painfully watched through the apartment window as my husband plodded with his load. With heaving sobs he cradled the jacket, kissed it, and buried his head in it. Finally, with great effort, he parted with it. "Hell on earth" seemed to best describe that moment, still vivid in my memory.

We took a walk, just the two of us. "It's such a beautiful day," I wailed, "but I cannot see or feel beauty. You

43

could put me in the middle of the Swiss Alps, and I would see no beauty."

"And there is not a single piece of music that appeals to me," Dale replied. Deep sorrow is frightening. For the first time in our married life, we were powerless to help each other. Each of us was fighting for survival.

"The LORD is near to the brokenhearted, and saves the crushed in spirit" (Ps. 34:18).

15

One Step Ahead

THE memorial service for Jack at the Palm Lane Church was magnificent. All three congregations with whom Jack and Kathy were affiliated were involved in the service. The church was filled, with many of the same people there who had supported us in the waiting room of the hospital. The atmosphere was alive with emotion and love, and we felt comforted.

Each of three pastors delivered a brief, Christ-centered meditation. We found consolation in their scriptural emphasis and their personal approach. At times they spoke directly to us, the family. They acknowledged Jack's committed-Christian lifestyle. Aware that some in attendance were not professing Christians, they seized the opportunity to present Christ as the only way of salvation.

The Baptist pastor closed his meditation by relating a recent conversation in which he had questioned Jack about his plans for the future. Jack replied, "Pastor, I'm not sure, but I do know one thing: The Lord has always been one step ahead of me."

With a huge smile, the pastor affirmed, "Jack, now you are one step ahead of all of us!"

The Arizona State Graduate Chorale participated in the service, the same group that two weeks before had sung for Jack's doctoral recital.

A fellow graduate student read a letter she had written titled "Jack Made the Difference," paying tribute to "his kindness, his sense of humor, his conservative nature, his creative spirit, and his strong belief in God." There was a long silence as she struggled for control. Through

45

her tears she concluded, "The hardest thing of all to accept is the fact that we never got to say good-bye. None of us had the opportunity to say, 'Jack, we think you're special, thanks for everything, and we love you.'"

Howard Vos, professor of physics at Arizona State University and member of the Palm Lane Church, wrote and read "Eulogy for Jack Grotenhuis":

We have known Jack for such a little while, but it is a blessing nonetheless. We were blessed with a God-given talent, and we saw the promise of a great career of service to the church of God, especially in the music of the church. We caught a glimpse of a mind that would have produced heavenly music and taught generations of God's people to sing and play his praises in new and wonderful ways. We had a fleeting moment in which we saw how he could inspire [children] and adults to do their very best with their talents.

We need someone new to help us hear a little of heaven while we are still here.
We need someone new who will drive himself toward uncompromising excellence while being pleased with a best try from others.
We need someone new to inspire our confidence.
We need someone new to help us see what we can do.

The lilting laugh is a memory.

The talented fingers are still.

The resonant voice is quiet.

The arms and hands direct no more.

The creative mind is resting.

46

Our heavenly Father has need of this devoted,
talented man in the greatest of all choirs. We
reluctantly but confidently give him back to the
giver of all good and perfect gifts.
Jack, we were just getting to know you.

The service ended with a recording of "The Lord Is My
Shepherd," a duet sung by Jack and Kathy just a few
months before his death. No one could mistake his resonant voice ringing through the sanctuary: "and I shall
dwell in the house of the Lord forever."

Jack would have loved his own memorial service. We
were overwhelmed with the outpouring of love for him and
for us, his parents. Thank God for this warm memory!

"Surely goodness and mercy shall follow me all the
days of my life; and I shall dwell in the house of the
LORD for ever" (Ps. 23:6).

16

Homecoming

BECAUSE the plane was half-empty when we departed Phoenix Saturday noon, the five of us—Dale and I, Kathy, Laurie, and Ellis—sat separately. We were exhausted and deeply grieved, and each of us felt the need to be alone. I took one last look at the city as we flew over the university campus, the mountains Jack had loved with a passion, and the contrasting desert. Goodbye Phoenix, city of sorrow, city of brotherly love!

What seemed to be a misfortune was God's perfect planning. The midwest was having a sleet storm, and we were the last plane allowed to land in Omaha. We slid down the runway, took a limousine to a nearby motor inn, and were unexpectedly stranded there for the night. God knew we needed to have our "batteries" recharged before we reached Sioux Center.

The five of us had dinner together, shared evening devotions, and spent a few warm and relaxing moments in the jacuzzi, sans bathing suits! One gentleman obligingly left the pool area when he saw that we were wearing only the barest essentials. A certain perversity took over. I didn't care about proper attire. I reckon I didn't care about anything.

We arrived at home around suppertime Sunday evening and were met at the door by our three boys and our dear friends, Howard and Vicki Hall. What a loving homecoming! Candles were burning, and a buffet supper was on the dining room table. Our retired college president led us in our suppertime devotions. Home—our haven of refuge!

48

Then we were called to the telephone. It was the local funeral home, informing us they were ready to pick up Jack's body from a nearby airport where it had arrived from Phoenix. He had indeed come home, but in a casket! I hit bottom; it was the lowest moment in my entire life.

Son Bob put his arms around me. "I love you, Mom," he assured me. But I was like Rachel, "refusing to be comforted." My twenty-five-year-old son needed something from me in return, and I did not give it. That was a mistake, and I am terribly sorry.

"God is our refuge and strength, a very present help in trouble" (Ps. 46:1).

17

Shadow of Death

Not wishing to do Jack an injustice, we decided to have a closed casket and have never regretted that decision. The length of time between his accident and his burial was a prohibitive factor to an open casket. His brothers and his relatives did not see his body, and later that was to bother me. However, they have overruled my misgivings, wishing to remember Jack as he was in life, not in death.

We were touched by the numerous flowers and plants sent to the funeral home from several parts of the country. Two large bouquets flanking Jack's casket were for "Teacher, Friend" from the band and choir of Lynden Christian High School in Lynden, Washington, where Jack spent his first two years of teaching.

We were sustained at the funeral home by the presence in the receiving line of our families, Kathy and her parents, and Jack's grandparents. We greeted many hundreds of people from both the Dordt College faculty and student body, and the Sioux Center community.

The Dordt College choir entered the funeral home as a group. On each face I saw love and fear, as if to convey "We don't know what to say or how to help you."

Most people expressed a sincere sympathy, many with empathetic tears. Some just grabbed our hands and gave us long, soulful gazes. One Dordt student carried a long-stemmed red rose which he tenderly placed on top of the casket. I was deeply moved by that gesture. One couple whispered in my ear, "You may count your blessings," and I later learned that they were the parents of a motorcycle accident victim who survived, but with severe mental and physical impairments.

Another well-meaning friend said, "You know, Eleanor, that 'all things work together for good to those who love God.'"

I answered honestly, "Yes, I know that in my head, but not in my heart. God will, I trust, make that clear to me." Those folks could go home and have dinner with *all* of their children seated around the table. We must be careful when we glibly quote Scripture in times such as these, because it can lay a guilt trip on the bereaved.

Most helpful to me was the gentleman who took both of my hands, looked at me eyeball to eyeball, and confidently stated, "One thing I know about you. You are a survivor!" He restored my shaky self-confidence.

God had us by the hand, leading us gently "through the valley of the shadow of death." Of that we were certain. We were going to survive, not because of who *we* were but because of who *God* is.

"Even though I walk through the valley of the shadow of death, I fear no evil; for thou art with me" (Ps. 23:4).

18

Song of Triumph

"Great and wonderful are thy deeds,
O Lord God the Almighty!
Just and true are thy ways, O King of the ages!
Who shall not fear and glorify thy name, O Lord?
For thou alone art holy" (Rev. 15:2–4).

WHEN the pastor read these beautiful words at the pre-funeral family service, I nudged my husband and whispered, "This must be the text for your next anthem. You could call it 'The Song of Triumph.'" Dale nodded apathetically. I was fearful that he would never again have the desire to compose music, knowing that a part of him had died with Jack. I prayed that our son's death would not paralyze his father's compositional skills.

God answered that prayer. The seeds were planted, and two days after the funeral, God inspired Dale to write "Song of Triumph." With broken heart he worked nonstop for sixteen hours in the privacy of his college office. Carrying the completed composition, he returned home like a conquering hero. We were both elated in the midst of deep sorrow. God's power had enabled him to "do far more abundantly than all that we ask or think" (Eph. 3:20).

The subsequent history of this choral anthem alone could fill a book. It was first introduced to hundreds of choral directors at a summer convention at the University of Missouri. Dale was asked to give the background of the composition, a remarkable God-given opportunity to speak of God's faithfulness. There was not a dry eye in the auditorium. To this day those musicians speak of the impact of Dale's testimony on their lives.

Six months later on their worldwide tour, the famed Norman Luboff Choir performed "Song of Triumph." Soon after, it was published by the Boosey and Hawkes Publishing Company, and the anthem is one of their most widely sung compositions.

The University of Southern California choir also sang this memorial anthem on their world tour. In their final performance in the massive Dom (cathedral) in Cologne, Germany, they combined with several European choirs. When given the opportunity to select their favorite anthem as a grand finale, the singers chose "Song of Triumph."

One of my support-group friends lost her sixteen-year-old daughter, Carol, to cancer. Shortly before she died, this perceptive child asked, "Mother, six months from now, who will remember that I lived?" That statement, made by a young girl I never knew, has motivated us to create music and write a book. Thus, Jack's memory lives on in our celebration of God's great and wonderful deeds as we have seen them through the life and death of our son.

19

Child of God, Member of God's Family

"HAVING been raised as a child of . . . God in a Christian family, my. . . world-and-life view runs deep. It is a scriptural view of God, man, creation, and their interrelationships. Both my wife and I are committed Christians, eager to seek and do God's will." So wrote Jack in his personal statement, when he applied for a teaching position at Dordt College.

"A child of God"—words of hope and comfort. The funeral service was a visible picture of the extended Christian family as we sat together. My mother and father, who expected to reach glory long before Jack, had lost their eldest grandson. Jack had spent many hours discussing theology with his minister-grandfather. His grandparents played a strategic role in his spiritual growth and strong Christian principles. Now they had double grief: the loss of Jack, and the feeling of helplessness as they watched us, their children, suffer. Grampa and Gramma Grotenhuis, long deceased, were spared this pain.

The funeral service, conducted by our college president, had dignity. He encouraged us to look up and ahead with resurrection expectation. The music was splendid. When the voices of the Dordt choir floated over the audience from the back of the sanctuary, Dale's eyes filled. "All I hear is *soul*," he whispered to me. That statement was the finest tribute any choir could receive from their director.

We made our way to the narthex of the church, awaiting transportation to the cemetery. An uncontrollable yearning for a last look at Jack made me break line, run to the closed casket, and hug his picture to my breast. I returned to my place and only then noticed that the Dordt choir had witnessed this desperate gesture. I saw sheer terror on their faces and I mouthed, "I love you" through the glass partition. "I love you, too," they responded tearfully.

We made our way to the cemetery, through the wide streets of this small town Jack had loved, past his elementary school, past a larger church with prominent steeple and illuminated cross. The trees drooped over the narrow drive to the grave as if to say, "We mourn too." On that cold December day we committed Jack to the grave.

Jack's maternal grandparents later bought his gravestone as their memorial gift. It reads: "Behold, I have engraved you on the palms of my hands." Many times Jack had declared, "Grampa, of all the sermons I have heard you preach, that is my favorite."

Feeling empty and totally drained, we left the cemetery. Good-bye, precious one. Lord, hasten the day when we shall be reunited.

"For the promise is to you and to your children and to all that are far off, every one whom the Lord our God calls to him" (Acts 2:39).

Part Three

Who will not fear you, O Lord, and bring glory to your name?

20

Baby Steps

An immediate need of the relative or friend of a grieving person is to pray that God bestows a rich measure of understanding, patience, and love. Bereaved individuals sometimes act and speak in bizarre ways in an attempt to ease their debilitating pain.

We returned to our home after the postfuneral luncheon. Dad's request was a reasonable one. "Eleanor, sit down and let's talk," he urged.

"Dad," I impatiently answered, "I have talked for a week straight and I can't say one more word!" Emotionally spent, I climbed the stairs to our bedroom and found my sister crying on the bed. I went to our basement apartment and discovered my brother weeping in solitude. There was no place to be alone in my own house!

I solved the dilemma by donning my most faded pair of jeans and an old blouse and proceeded to dust and vacuum the entire upstairs while all of the people I loved best were conversing downstairs. As I scrubbed the bathroom floor I took comfort in the fact that I had taken the first baby step toward rehabilitation. While lacking in social grace, this gesture was therapeutic for me. Every aspect of my life was out of order, but in this insignificant area I had a semblance of control and a sense of accomplishment. At that point it was about all I could do.

I loved my family and friends for giving me my space.

"A friend loves at all times" (Prov. 17:17 NIV).

21

We Still Have Each Other

THERE was a series of good-byes as family and friends left for their respective homes. Bob returned to his television job, and Phil to his college apartment to begin studying for final exams. Kathy remained with us for an additional week. The house was suddenly very quiet. It was all over. It seemed that life itself was over.

How wonderful it felt to be alone and sleeping in our own bed! For a long time we did not speak; we just hugged tightly. Finally Dale said, "You know that I loved that boy with all of my soul, but I love you infinitely more. We still have each other."

I have long remembered and clung to those sensitive and endearing words.

"Love one another as I have loved you" (John 15:12).

22

Face of Duty

MOST choral directors have at one time or another faced a "show-must-go-on" situation. I wonder how many conductors have faced a choir of over one hundred members and a chamber orchestra as Dale did only five days after he buried his son.

Only his chalk-white face betrayed his frailty as he walked onstage and acknowledged the vigorous and empathetic applause. The Dordt College chapel-auditorium was packed to capacity for the choral Christmas concert. Fifteen hundred people were unusually quiet. The air was filled with a tension that seemed to convey from every person: "If I don't move, and sit very straight, maybe this man won't collapse." I thanked God for our loving and supportive community.

My husband deserved a medal for courage and decorum in the face of duty. It was a beautiful, God-glorifying afternoon. My thoughts often went to Jack, already singing in the celestial choir. Afterward Dale confessed to me, "I remember nothing, saw no one. But I didn't miss a cue, because God conducted this concert for me."

We gathered with the choir members for postconcert devotions and parting words, as they were about to enjoy their Christmas vacation. We both felt the need to talk heart to heart with this group of lovable, impressionable young people. To illustrate our dual concern for their safety and their salvation, we took the liberty of reading to them excerpts from letters Jack had written to us from graduate school. At the time, he was still single, working on his master's degree, and living in a Christian co-op house. Choir members listened intently as I read:

> Here are a couple of interesting things that should make you feel good. Ruth (fellow student) asked me to lead this week's discussion on a book we're all reading, a Christian book on the Christian life and its struggles called *The Fight,* by John White. I read about halfway through the chapter and told her that I couldn't lead it, but would be willing to lead any other chapter in the book. The title was "Changed Relationships," and it dealt with some of the struggles new Christians go through when they're converted and the rest of the family isn't Christian. I had to tell Ruth that I couldn't relate to any part of what I'd read, because a) I never was "converted" and always considered myself [a child of God], and b) my parents and the rest of the family were Christian, and there were no hassles about bringing the faith to other family members.
>
> While we were talking about parents, Ruth said she envied me because it seemed from the way I talked that I got along with my folks so well. Then she reminded me of one of our first house meetings, when we were all asked who our heroes were, or who we at least looked up to the most. She reminded me that when asked who the most influential people were in my life and who I looked up to the most, I replied, "My folks." She said she really thought that was quite something.
>
> P.S. Say, thanks for the ten dollars you sent, for the $150 you lent me for the trip to Calgary, and for letting me put a full tank of gas on your co-op bill. All things considered, you're the best folks any guy could have.

The point was not that we were deserving of these accolades, but to ask these students, with some urgency, "If you met with an accident like Jack did, are you assured of your salvation? Have you assured your family? Have you ever thanked your parents or expressed your love to them? Don't wait; do it now. Life can be very short!"

Judging from the student and parental response, the conversation bore fruit. Several of Dale's students have said, "My life changed the day you lost Jack." Only later did I recall what I said to Kathy as we left the hospital in Phoenix: "Kathy, if one person would come to know the Lord through Jack's death, Jack would say it was worth it all."

"Behold, you have instructed many, and you have strengthened the weak hands. Your words have upheld him who was stumbling, and you have made firm the feeble knees" (Job 4:34).

23

Merry Christmas

CHRISTMAS 1983 came, two weeks after Jack's death. We began the day in God's house, and that was good. We needed to see Jesus; we needed to be with his people.

My mind wandered during the service, for I was thinking about Jack. He was spending Christmas in heaven with his Redeemer, with Jesus, who is our only hope of life eternal. I wondered what heaven is like on Christmas morning. Does the celestial choir participate in a heavenwide celebration? Do the angels sing "glory to God in the highest" as they did the first Christmas? What do glorified, perfect voices sound like? An ethereal sound, no doubt. Maybe someday I will sit in the "heavenly bleachers" and watch Jack and his earthly father co-conduct a major work, something they dreamed about but could not accomplish while on this earth.

My abominable pain brought me back to reality. My face felt hot and my eyes stung. I felt claustrophobic in the midst of so many people. It was difficult to concentrate for any length of time. We obviously were an emotionally damaged family. Phil seemed grim and sad; Tom was bewildered and clung to his dad; Dale wept almost nonstop. I prayed to God to help us through that painful day.

"Merry Christmas," said a well-meaning church member as we walked out of church. It would have been far more helpful to me if she had squeezed my hand and said, "We'll be praying for you today." We enviously observed that our neighbors' driveways were occupied with the cars of their children and other relatives. Their homes, undoubtedly, were filled with laughter. Ours was not. The television screen, magazine ads, and Christmas cards were stabbing reminders that our family was not intact. Phil insisted on taking us out for a prime rib dinner in a small nearby cafe, and we were the sole occupants. But that beat sitting around the table at home mindful of the empty chairs.

Jack, being the oldest, was always the pacesetter for our holiday activities, saying, "Let's see slides," or "Let's play Pit," or "Let's make homemade ice cream."

Now Phil took over. "Let's go bowling, then come home and open gifts." We sadly but lovingly opened our gifts. Those intended for Jack were stored in a closet.

At bedtime we felt we had achieved our goal—to survive the day. But there was more. Through the blur of tears we did see Jesus and our love for each other. So ended Christmas 1983, for us, a painful memory.

The Christmas 1983 story does not end here, however. Since then we have made tremendous strides in coping with the holidays, but it has taken considerable effort and planning.

I vividly recall Christmas 1988 as a turning point. I was shopping and had just purchased a sweater. As I left the store, the clerk wished me a merry Christmas. Looking her in the eye with an enthusiastic lilt to my voice, I answered, "And you, too. I hope you have a wonderful holiday." I *meant* it.

Suddenly the music in the mall made me smile, the decorations looked lovely, and I felt lighthearted. I leaned against the outside of the store and breathed deeply. "Thank you, Lord, for this momentous experience." I was healing at last!

A key to coping with the holidays lies in advance planning. I suggest the following:

1. Lean heavily on God through prayer and time with his Word.

2. Focus on your *living* loved ones. Think about what you will *do*, not of how you may *feel*.
3. Plan to be with people you enjoy.
4. Consider changing some of your family traditions—the time of your dinner, the time and place of gift exchange, your family activities.
5. Consider a family excursion or happening—sledding, taking a walk in the woods, attending a concert or play, making a short trip, creating a new experience in a different place.
6. Don't be afraid to express your feelings, to talk about the deceased. Relive the happy memories inwardly and aloud.
7. Buy flowers for your church or home in memory of your loved one.
8. Reach out. Visit your hospital nursing wing, share your home with those lonelier than you, deliver a few plates of homemade anything to someone who needs them far worse than you do.
9. Allow yourself "letting go" time and a balance of solitude and sociability.
10. Memorize and live the "Serenity Prayer": God, give me the serenity to accept the things I cannot change, courage to change the things I can, and wisdom to know the difference.

Henry Ford said, "Think you can, think you can't. Either way, you're right." I have used this quotation often as a leader of a weight-loss organization. The same applies to the griever dealing with the built-in difficulties of the holiday season.

"For I will restore health to you, and your wounds I will heal" (Jer. 30:17).

24

What Faults?

"Mom," asked son Phil, with an affectionate twinkle in his eye, "when you write about Jack, are you going to mention his faults?"

I admit that my first impulse was to arch my back and snap, "What faults?" But I smiled and replied, "Of course." Bereaved people almost universally admit that there is a tendency to bestow sainthood upon the deceased. I find it difficult, almost disloyal, to write about Jack's faults, but would find it equally so to discuss the weaknesses of our remaining three sons. Therapists believe that when we can finally acknowledge the faults of the departed, we are beginning to heal.

Let me emphasize that Jack's death was not a result of his own negligence. We are thankful for that. Yet there was always a streak of immaturity in him. He drove his car with a vengeance, climbed too steep foothills with his motorcycle, swam too long distances in too deep reservoirs, canoed in wild rapids, hiked in remote mountain territory, and skied almost maniacally. This boyish recklessness was in direct contrast to his unusual level of spiritual maturity.

Friends remember his opinionated nature. His theological and philosophical views tended to be black or white. His various writings reflected his strong convictions and low tolerance for the opposing view. Graduate school mellowed him somewhat, though all of his colleagues describe him as a person with strong principles.

Jack lived zestfully and intensely, as if he knew that life for him would be brief. There was an impatience about him. "Life is so short" was his excuse for doing what was often impractical.

I am sure that if Jack could speak from heaven he would remind us: "Don't forget for one moment that I was a sinner, saved by grace alone." Romans 8 was his favorite chapter in Scripture. He especially loved verse 1: "There is therefore now no condemnation for those who are in Christ Jesus."

God forbid that we should cling to anyone or anything other than the cross of Christ!

"For by grace you have been saved through faith; and this is not your own doing, it is the gift of God—not because of works, lest any man should boast" (Eph. 2:8–9).

25

Absence Is Like the Sky

WE learned that grief is complicated and multifaceted. We were in a deep depression, consumed by feelings of helplessness and hopelessness. Zest for life, optimism, and sense of well-being ceased to exist. "What is the use of going on?" we asked each other.

We were plagued physically with fatigue and lethargy. Minor chores took supreme effort as we moved with numb hands and leaden feet. We experienced ulcerlike pain in the upper abdomen. Extreme stress and sorrow had affected Dale's salivary glands, and his tongue stuck to the roof of his mouth. More than one person honestly expressed to us, "You've aged!"

We were affected mentally. We could not concentrate and seemed unable to remember from one moment to the next. Making any kind of a decision was difficult. Planning and carrying out the plan was a formidable task. Lacking confidence and control, we felt ill equipped for day-to-day living and all of its responsibilities.

We were on an emotional teeter-totter. At times shock mercifully enfolded me, and Jack's death did not seem real. Perhaps it is a bad dream, I inwardly argued. I forced myself to stand before a mirror and command, "Repeat after me: Jack is dead!" Ultimately reality hit. I would never see him again in this life. The truth was more than I could bear. I collapsed in a heap and groaned in a voice that I did not recognize.

Now I understand the meaning of the "valley of the shadow of death." I could not seem to crawl out of that valley. The loss of Jack had become an obsession. I "saw" his face, "heard" his voice, "felt" his presence. I could not let go. Deep grief hung like an albatross around my neck, squeezing the life out of me like a giant boa constrictor. I was s l o w l y sinking into the quicksand of despair. What should I do? Where could I go? How would I survive?

C. S. Lewis said it best when referring to his deceased wife: "Her absence is like the sky—it covers everything." I was enveloped in a thick fog, a dark grey world. I knew that above the fog was a deep blue sky and a blazing sun, but I could not see it.

The Holy Spirit finally nudged me to God's Word for help. Many passages took on new significance, spoke to me and all of us in bold, large lettering for our comfort. Even in that dark moment I was able by God's grace to acknowledge comfort from his Word as one of the blessings in grief for the child of God.

Grief may be complicated, but recovery will depend on two prerequisites: *faith* and *obedience*. I had finally begun to learn—the hard way—the full implications of those two vitally important words.

"Why are you cast down, O my soul, and why are you disquieted within me? Hope in God; for I shall again praise him, my help and my God" (Ps. 42:5).

26

State of Being

ONE evening in May 1984 we returned to our hotel room in Groningen, The Netherlands. The Dordt College Choir had just performed in the massive and marvelous Martinikerk to a large and appreciative audience.

"How do you feel, hon?" I ask my weary director-husband.

"I feel that one of these nights my limbs are going to come out of their sockets as I conduct. Truthfully, I'm hanging by a thread. And what about you?"

"I'm not much better," I replied. "I'm walking on the very edge of the Grand Canyon. I look down, and it is deep and dark. The slightest breeze would blow me into the abyss."

It was an honest assessment of our state of being, and admitting it was therapeutic. We were no longer in the shock stage but were dealing with harsh reality. We smiled ruefully at ourselves—two weak and fragile people responsible for a college choir tour in Europe only five months after Jack's death. How thankful we were for the love and support of our beloved choir members!

God's presence and power continued to amaze us, flowing like the widow's oil, never ceasing and always in super abundance. We talked of that, and then we slept in peace.

"He gives power to the faint, and to him who has no might he increases strength" (Isa. 40:29).

27

Begging for Comfort

GRIEF is humbling! Bereaved people are like helpless beggars, holding out their tin cups, pleading not for pennies but for comfort. They are lonely and desperate. Pastors, church council members, fellow believers, colleagues, co-workers—please don't walk past them. Put something into their tin cups.

Some time ago I listened to a chaplain from a mental health institute speak on the stages of grief. He had lost his son three years prior and was still struggling with anger. Clenching his fists and gritting his teeth he declared, "I am here to say that the church was a dismal failure." Would that be true of other churches?

Grievers often make nongrievers uncomfortable. They feel fearful and inadequate to the task of consoling. It is safer to walk across the street than to face the bereaved. It is better, people believe, to say nothing than to express something inane or counterproductive. But those who grieve do understand how difficult it is for others to deal with them.

Based on our experience, our family has developed the following suggestions to those who would console the bereaved:

1. Don't say "I know how you feel" if you haven't lost a child.
2. Don't expect more of us than we are able to give. Allow us time to grieve. Give us the option of saying, "No, I am not up to this," without our feeling guilty.

3. Don't say, "Call me if you need me."
4. Don't preach to us about self-pity, letting go, or getting over it. We will never be "over it."
5. Don't ask us how we are doing and go on talking about something else before we can answer.
6. Don't avoid meeting us face to face, even though doing so may be uncomfortable for you. We cannot bear being shunned.
7. Do squeeze our hands or put your arms around our shoulders. We need your touch.
8. Do let us cry when we have the need.
9. Do remember that talking is not essential. Your presence shows that you care. We can read sympathy in your eyes.
10. Do continue praying for us. We need the prayers of God's people and sense when they diminish.
11. Do follow that impulse to bring over a pot of soup, or a plate of muffins, or a hot dish. Cooking is a formidable task during those first weeks.
12. Do call us and assure us of your thoughts and prayers.
13. Do send short notes in the mail. They have made many a day for us.
14. Do forgive us when we extol or even exaggerate the virtues of our loved one.
15. Do talk to us about our beloved. Recall memories, make us smile with humorous anecdotes. Please let us know that you have not forgotten him.

Pastors, council members, fellow believers—we need your compassionate ministry. Your quiet presence sustains us. Your aid in making decisions is invaluable. Take our hands as you pray with us. Encourage us with a few choice verses from Scripture, but be brief; our stunned minds cannot grasp more than two or three main thoughts. Tell us about God, bring us to the cross of Christ. Reassure us of the Spirit's groaning in our behalf.

Remember that though the funeral is over, our walk down this devastating road has just begun. It gets worse before it gets better, so don't let go of us too soon.

"Have pity on me, have pity on me, O you my friends, for the hand of God has touched me!" (Job 19:21).

28

The Other Children

YES, what about the other children? Too often they are forgotten or brushed aside. Writing this chapter is difficult, because I have pangs of regret. I wish I had known what I do now. Bemoaning what might have been is futile, except that my writing this may help someone else.

When we returned from Phoenix we were greeted by a houseful of family and friends. We faced decisions and social obligations. I wish we first had regrouped as an immediate family to share our emotions and weep together. We should have spent time alone to express our love and appreciation for each other, to pledge our mutual support, and to emphatically confirm to our three remaining boys that each one was our "favorite." I wish we had prayed together and reaffirmed our faith and trust in God. I'm sorry for these omissions.

Outwardly Dale and I subdued much of our grief to create a reasonably pleasant home for the rest of our family. When ten-year-old Tom came home from school, I would quickly dry my tears, force a smile, and ask about his day. It would have been far more healthy to weep in front of him occasionally, teaching him that it's okay to cry when you're sad. I should have encouraged him to release his feelings and expressed mine. Interestingly, he was not deceived by our Herculean efforts to be optimistic. His memory: "Our house was sad for so long." Tom lived in an atmosphere of anxiety and depression during his most formative years. It took its toll.

Phil, six years younger than Jack, changed radically through this experience. He felt a pressure not so much to achieve as to enter a life of serving the Lord. He was a journalism major and expressed his feelings on paper. He frequented Jack's grave. He took long walks with Joy (now his wife), talked freely, and shed tears. Of our home he says, "It was not morbid; our family was not torn apart. But we never knew how you and Dad were doing." Honesty would have been the best policy.

Bob, as an NBC television newscaster, has mastered the art of covering tragic news with seeming objectivity and control. This tragedy was different. He lost his brother with whom he had played (and occasionally fought) most of his life. Though different in temperament and interests, they were intensely loyal to each other. Bob respected Jack's abilities and Christian principles and lamented to his grandfather, "It should have been me. On the other hand, Jack was twenty years ahead of me on the road to sanctification. I just wish I had called out to him, as Elisha to Elijah: 'Let me inherit a double portion of your spirit'" (2 Kings 2:9 NIV).

Bob was carrying a heavy load of mixed feelings. One of them was a profound regret mixed with a bit of resentment that we did not encourage him to fly to Phoenix when Jack was injured. He feels he was deprived of the opportunity to say good-bye to his brother. He also feels that this had adverse implications for his grief process. He delayed his grief for months—no, years. "Mom," he admitted recently, "almost as painful to me as Jack's death was to helplessly stand by and watch you and Dad suffer so intensely." He felt an obligation to be a bulwark for us. He has yet to visit his brother's grave.

On the sixth anniversary of Jack's death Bob telephoned me from Boise, Idaho, where he was working. He sounded like my son, not a television news anchor. He asked how I was feeling and then confided, "Today I am very depressed. I know I should rejoice because Jack is in glory, but I can only think of the void in my life without him and what our whole family has lost." Six years! He was at long last beginning to come to terms with his grief. Allow me these observations:

1. Idealizing the memory of a dead child can be harmful to the siblings, leaving an I'll-never-measure-up complex. We want to guard against two extreme reactions; rebellion or a fade-into-the-woodwork withdrawal.
2. Overprotecting the other children, both physically and emotionally, creates an atmosphere of insecurity and anxiety.
3. Showing vulnerability and talking about it is not a sign of weakness.
4. There is no correct way to grieve. Not crying does not mean not caring. Children must be allowed their time, manner, and space to grieve, just as parents demand them for themselves.

Could I have done differently? I am not sure. There was so much pain that I felt unable to be a sensitive and perceptive parent. In all the numbness and confusion, I did my best. God graciously took care of the rest.

"But where shall wisdom be found? And where is the place of understanding?" (Job 28:12).

29

Time to Grieve

I will remember January 19, 1984, for its pain. It was the day Jack was scheduled to be interviewed for a position in the Dordt College music department. That night it seemed as though he had never lived.

Like characters in a play we greeted the two fine musicians who were interviewed in his place. Along with several other faculty members we attended a lovely reception in their honor. A feeling of acute deprivation seized me as I struggled to be gracious, to smile, to converse. Jack's absence hung over me like a canopy. My soul bled all evening over "what might have been." I silently and resentfully wondered why we were expected to attend an event that would obviously be extremely painful.

In our efforts to rise to the expectations of others and to be responsible to our many duties, we neither took nor asked for the time to grieve. Instead, we relentlessly forged ahead and overcompensated, paying the price physically and emotionally in ensuing months.

Because we were inexperienced mourners we gave no thought to "healthy" or "unhealthy" grieving. For a long period of time we were intent on mere survival of each day and nothing more. Now we can only hope to warn and help others through the potential pitfalls on the road to recovery.

Do take the time to grieve!

"Lord, all my longing is known to thee, my sighing is not hidden from thee. My heart throbs, my strength fails me" (Ps. 38:9).

77

30

Punishment? No!

WHEN I reflect on Jack as a musician and an educator, when I contemplate his uncommon interest in theology and his love for God, then when I observe his college friends conducting concerts, serving as church officers, enjoying life as happy husbands and fathers, I ask, Why, why, why?

Returning home after the funeral, Jack's young wife said, "Mom and Dad, *I* don't know why, but God knows why, and that's enough for me." Does that statement of faith and obedience sound too simple? It *is* simple. The answer to why? is: "Be still and know that I am God" (Ps. 46:10). This means that God's purposes for Jack's life (and many like him) were accomplished. Period. His death was not a mistake nor flawed judgment, but perfect timing. "For he will complete what he appoints for me" (Job 23:14).

One of my acquaintances suggested, "Maybe you loved your son too much and that is why God took him." One of Dale's respected professional friends offered, "I hate to tell you this Dale, but your son must have committed some terrible sin, and God is punishing him." Neither of these people meant to inflict hurt, but both suffer from faulty theology.

Consider John 9:1–3: "As he passed by, he saw a man blind from his birth. And his disciples asked him, 'Rabbi, who sinned, this man or his parents, that he was born blind?' Jesus answered, 'It was not that this man sinned, or his parents, but that the works of God might be made manifest in him.'"

Though death is a result of sin, Satan did not cause Jack's death. God orchestrates all events and circumstances in our lives. "I know, O LORD, that thy judgments are right, and that in faithfulness thou hast afflicted me" (Ps. 119:75).

Furthermore, God does not use trials to punish us for our sins. To chasten and discipline, yes; to punish, no. Christ took *all* our deserved punishment and paid for *all* our sins (past, present, and future) on the cross. We are forgiven. Amazingly, God has forgotten what he has forgiven. This is grace. Because Jesus suffered and died on the cross, arose and ascended into heaven, we suffer victoriously.

"For I will be merciful toward their iniquities, and I will remember their sins no more" (Heb. 8:12).

31

Dreams

I awoke from a deep sleep to hear my husband's whimpering. I knew the reason, as usual. His recurring dream seemed so real.

In it Jack was alive. He would be standing at the foot of our bed, smiling serenely with a faraway look in his eye. When Dale longingly reached for him, Jack would gently say, "I must go to my Father." Without looking back, he would walk purposefully toward a blinding light. The experience was both painful and comforting to Dale.

Just recently I experienced my only dream of Jack. In it we were filing out of the Dordt College chapel-auditorium, and Jack was frantically searching the crowd for Kathy. (She has remarried.) "Jack," I urged, "don't look any longer. It's for the best." He nodded.

Then I hesitantly asked, "Jack, now that you're back, what is going to happen to all of the good changes in our lives *because* you died?" The dream suddenly ended with that heavy question.

I cannot begin to express how we long to see our son! But I never want to be asked, "Would you sacrifice these monumental inner changes to have him back?"

"Count it all joy, my brethren, when you meet various trials, for you know that the testing of your faith produces steadfastness. And let steadfastness have its full effect" (James 1:2–4).

32

Work to Do

OFTEN we have prayed these prayers:

Father, your will be done.
Refine, purify, change me.
Lord, conform me to your image.
Enable me to be your servant.
How can I best serve you? Show me! Use me!

God has answered those prayers in more unexpected and grindingly difficult ways than we could ever have imagined.

Within five weeks of Jack's death, God led me to a busy speaking ministry. I view these opportunities as God's gift to me on a silver platter, because they have been strategic to my recovery. God forced me to reach out, to use this sad experience to help others, and to glorify him. In my feeble attempts to give, I have received an hundredfold. He has kept me through many miles of travel and placed hundreds of hurting, magnificent people in my life and continues to do so. Our wise and loving God has ushered both Dale and me into our uniquely private "mission fields."

There seems to be no end to the opportunities to "comfort those who are in any affliction" (2 Cor. 1:4). I am utterly amazed that God would choose such a weak vessel as I for this awesome responsibility. I am accountable for all of these God-given opportunities. God, be merciful to me.

I often talk to myself. (My family teases me about this.) As I prepare for another speaking engagement, I tuck my speech and Jack's 8" x 10" portrait into my tote bag and say aloud, "Come, Jack, you and I have work to do."

A friend cautiously said, "Perhaps your son will accomplish more in his death than he would have in a normal lifetime." Maybe, but the very thought is difficult to contemplate.

"Blessed be the God and Father of our Lord Jesus Christ, the Father of mercies and God of all comfort, who comforts us in all our affliction, so that we may be able to comfort those who are in any affliction, with the comfort with which we ourselves are comforted by God" (2 Cor. 1:3, 4).

33

Laughter

I was totally engrossed in my morning devotions, talking openly and fervently with God. The telephone rang, and I hurried robotlike to answer.

"Lord," I absentmindedly greeted.

There was a brief silence, and then, "Oh, I'm afraid I have the wrong number," my dear friend nervously replied.

"Elsie, Elsie! Don't hang up!" I pleaded. "Would that we could receive a long-distance call from heaven."

I was embarrassed. We roared with laughter. God knew how badly I needed a good hearty laugh. A sense of humor is almost nonexistent in those early months of grief.

"He will yet fill your mouth with laughter, and your lips with shouting" (Job 8:21).

34

Treasures on Earth

"CLOTHES make the man." No one really believes that.
Yet we cannot disassociate clothes from specific individuals, especially one who has died. We kept postponing
the sorting and disposing of Jack's personal effects,
because we were not up to the task. It felt like a final dis-
posal of his *person.*

For several months our stomachs lurched at the sight
of two sizeable boxes of Jack's possessions. One wintry
night we attacked the sorting of their contents with deter-
mination. We decided that I would deal with Jack's
clothes, and Dale would sift through his piano, flute, and
oboe music, his voice books, and his musical arrange-
ments and original compositions.

We worked feverishly with our backs to each other.
We did not converse, but we sniffled continuously.
Sometimes we could not agree on whether to save or dis-
card. In our hurt we snapped impatiently at each other.
The job at last was finished—and so were we.

Dale carried the discarded items to our garage. But the
implications were far more than that. He brought his
musical legacy and his shattered dreams to the trash bar-
rel. I will always remember the sound of his anguished
cries cutting through the cold night air, penetrating the
sealed windows of our home and into my empathizing
heart. We have had the best of times. This was one of the
worst.

The following morning I watched soberly as the sani-
tation truck stopped to collect our garbage. The giant
teeth gobbled up and ground to shreds the contents of

the trash barrels—many of Jack's earthly possessions. God was teaching me another needed lesson: Where and to whom does *my* heart belong?

"Do not lay up for yourselves treasures on earth, but lay up for yourselves treasures in heaven"(Matt. 6:19, 20).

35

Long-Distance Call

My speaking engagement came to a close. As I gathered up my materials, a member of the audience tugged at my arm and asked if we could talk. She was red eyed and obviously distraught. "I'm having dreadful problems," she revealed. "I am responsible for the death of a little boy." Although she had been cleared of any fault in the accident, she nevertheless assumed responsibility for the tragedy. She was devastated.

We conversed at length. I experienced total emotional involvement. To this day she has no inkling of the lasting implications of our conversation. God used this openhearted woman to instill within me a deep compassion toward the young girl who had been involved in Jack's fatal accident. I resolved to call her as soon as possible. No doubt she, too, was suffering.

I searched for and found the accident report with her name, address, and telephone number. On a Sunday afternoon I called her Phoenix residence and identified myself to her father, who answered.

I sensed a distrust, then hesitation, and finally an open, rewarding communication. He revealed the psychological damage the accident had done to his daughter and her resulting inability to speak to me personally. God enabled me to assure him of our forgiveness, our Christian commitment, and our beliefs in a wise and loving God. I concluded with, "Tell her we are sorry and we bear no grudges."

Three months later Dale received a call from Phoenix at his Dordt College office. A weak, almost childlike voice said, "I am Lynn Harris (name changed). Your wife talked to my father and said she forgave me. Do you forgive me, too?" She sounded frail and pathetic.

Dale hastened to affirm his pardon and lovingly advised, "Now you must get on with your life." He was late for class and tearfully explained the reason for his tardiness. Both teacher and students learned more than music theory that day.

"Be merciful, even as your Father is merciful" (Luke 6:36).

36

Beauty Once More

I opened one eye. Instinct told me that something wonderful was about to happen. Our hotel room was bathed in a warm, pink glow. The purplish Alpine mountains were distinct against a cloudless sky. It was 5 A.M. Our Creator-God was nudging us. "Wake up," I whispered to Dale.

Sleep could indeed wait! I grabbed my camera and opened the door to our fifth floor balcony of the Hotel Europa on the shore of Lake Lugano. A breathless air of expectancy hovered over the glassy lake. One other member of our tour group gleefully waved to me from an adjoining balcony.

The scene was one of perfect quiet, serenity—a peace that had eluded us the past three long years. We savored and slowly digested every second. The countdown had begun. The sky changed from pink to bright red as the sun began its ascent. Click went my camera. Again. Once more!

Wonder of wonders, joy of joys! We had witnessed with our own eyes a glorious sunrise over the Swiss Alps. We beheld, and we tasted beauty once again.

"O LORD, our Lord, how majestic is thy name in all the earth!" (Ps. 8:1).

37

Marital Differences

"TILL death do us part" assumed a new significance, as losing Jack put a strain on our marriage. Anyone who believes that the loss of a child binds a couple together and strengthens a relationship should consider this statistic: Therese Goodrich, executive director of The Compassionate Friends, in Oak Brook, Illinois, a national group for parents who have suffered the death of a child, says most studies show 75 percent of couples experience significant marital problems.

After twenty-eight years of marvelous compatibility, deep sorrow began to accentuate the contrasts between our personalities. We grieved differently. I devoured numerous books about grief. They fortified me; these same books plunged Dale into despair. I needed change in environment; he needed the quiet comfort of home. I needed people; he needed privacy. Visiting Jack's grave was important to Dale; I could not bear the sight of our son's name engraved on that cold marble slab.

The simple logistics of our lives prevented our grieving simultaneously. I had the opportunity to explode in the daytime solitude of our home. My husband could unwind only at day's end, away from the control and personal charisma that his teaching responsibilities and choral conducting demanded. The result was that when *my* weeping had subsided, *his* had just begun.

Grief produces intolerable stress, and stress leads to undesirable changes. I saw my own weaknesses: pessimism, anxiety, short temper, impatience, and near-zero tolerance of anything and anyone. Like the apostle Paul,

I had to confess: "For I do not do the good I want, but the evil I do not want is what I do" (Rom. 7:19). I had neither the desire nor the energy to change, because I seemed to have died emotionally. I mentally pictured and envied the turtle who, at any time she pleases, can withdraw from the cruel world into her impenetrable shell. Isolation appealed to me. I did not have to face the world, and the world did not have to face me. In those early months I lacked the emotional health to nurture a marriage.

Paradoxically, the very qualities in our marriage that bind us—love, loyalty, honesty, sensitivity, open communication—were now secondary, while our protective instincts for each other became primary. Not wanting to compound each other's sorrow, we often kept our innermost thoughts and emotions from one another. My reasoning: "If I tell him how I really feel, I will add to his already heavy load." My husband's thinking: "She can't handle more. I won't bog her down with my difficulties."

The death of a child brings not only marriage, but every facet of the individual parent's life to a fork in the road. On trial are spiritual commitment, physical endurance, mental and emotional stability. How will we be remembered: bitter or better? paralyzed or productive?

The entire first year was a huge struggle to carry on with our personal lives and the tasks that God laid before us. We put into practice several of the concepts that I "preached" in my weight loss class.

"If you can't change the situation, change the way you respond to it." We opted to keep busy—in college-related activities, organizing an area support group for mothers who lost children, speaking, and continuing to host summer European tours for a travel agency. We realized the absolute necessity of staying in touch with the rest of humanity. Concerned about physical stamina, we ate balanced meals, watched our weight, and walked briskly on a regular basis.

"Plan ahead." We set aside time for ourselves. Only by leaving our home and community and staying a night or two in another city could we gain perspective and talk with a degree of objectivity. We enjoyed solitude and anonymity as we dined, shopped, read, or attended a concert. Those times were strategic to our marriage, though not without pain when we enviously observed happy young couples or whole families enjoying each other. Then, as now, the feeling of deprivation is our biggest struggle.

"Act the way you'd *like* to feel." What is so virtuous about smiling on the outside when you're crying on the inside? Sometimes the outward joy seeps subtly to the inside. With practice. For a long period of time our family gatherings around the dining room table seemed almost intolerable in spite of meticulous planning and brave attempts at optimism. Our family was not whole. Our joy was not complete. But Jesus was in that very room. He saw the empty chair. He, too, felt the ache, because his family, also, is incomplete. He understands the longing to be united. He prays: "Father, I desire that they also, whom thou hast given me, may be with me where I am, to behold my glory" (John 17:24). What a great consolation he can be to fragmented families everywhere!

The passing of the hours, days, and months brought gradual healing. Evening devotions continued to strengthen us as did long conversations over coffee. There was mutual support. The comfort of each other's arms sustained us. We can testify with Paul that we were "afflicted . . . but not crushed; perplexed, but not driven to despair; . . . struck down, but not destroyed. So we do not lose heart" (2 Cor. 4:8, 9, 16). Our marriage has survived the ultimate—the death of a child—but not without God's everlasting arms supporting us.

"But he knows the way that I take; when he has tried me, I shall come forth as gold" (Job 23:10).

91

Part Four

*You alone are holy . . .
your righteous acts
have been revealed*

38

Compensation for Loss

WE have a letter dated December 13, 1983, which reads:

Dear friends: We want to take this opportunity to express our deepest sympathy to you in the tragic loss of your son. We want you to know how sincerely grateful we are for my husband being the recipient of one of the kidneys. This will give him a new lease on life because of your thoughtfulness in allowing the kidneys to be used in a transplant. May the knowledge that you have allowed someone to be helped alleviate some of your grief. Again, we sincerely thank you. With heartfelt thanks, Lydia.

For nearly three years I thought of Lydia and her husband, who is living because our son Jack died. I wondered, Who are you? Where do you live? What do you do for a living? How were you selected as the recipient? Then, one day God allowed me to discover one of his answers. And that day he showed me: "So are my ways higher than your ways and my thoughts than your thoughts" (Isa. 55:9).

I kissed Dale good-bye at the airport on a warm October morning and boarded the plane. We had suffered much together, and I regretted that he would be unable to share this trip with me. I reached into my tote bag and removed my large red scrapbook. In it was the letter from Lydia, forwarded to us from the transplant center in Phoenix. The flight was smooth. I tried to absorb the full implications of the trip to Phoenix: I was on my way to see the man who lives because Jack died!

I recalled the events of the past week, which began with my phone call to the transplant center in Phoenix. Our name was familiar to the doctor in charge, because he had personally handled our case, and he quickly informed me of transplant policy: Transplant records are kept confidential. Mustering all of my courage, I argued that if adopted children could find their parents with the consent of both parties, why could not people like us glean beauty from something as devastating as the death of a young, promising son? The doctor was quiet. I persisted, saying that I, too, had a policy. Since our son had died, I had had a speaking ministry, talking to hundreds of young people, pleading with them to consider signing their names as potential organ donors on their next drivers' licenses. As a last-ditch attempt, I said to the doctor, "I have gone to bat for you; can't you do the same for me?"

"That seems reasonable," he replied, "and if you wait a moment, I will put his record on the computer." (Jack, a computer statistic!) But God was putting the pieces of this puzzle together. The doctor read the results of Jack's organ donation: One of Jack's kidneys was flourishing in the body of a man who lived in Payson, Arizona, eighty-five miles north of Phoenix. The doctor agreed to call this man, tell him my request, and ask him if he would like to meet me. He promised to call me back within the hour.

"Yes," came the doctor's answer, "he would like to meet you. Wait for his call." Then he said that the recipient was a Baptist minister. "A Baptist minister?" I literally shouted. "That's wonderful! We are Christians."

The doctor added, "These are God's mysterious ways."

I inquired further. Yes, this man was the husband of Lydia, but six months after the transplant Lydia had died, and the minister had since remarried. So Lydia, too, was in heaven.

Early the next morning the call came. A soft-spoken voice told me, "I had thought the Lord was calling me home, and instead he gave me new life through the death of your son."

I replied, "I know someone else who gave us life through his death, don't you? You are living with the kidney of a boy who loved the Lord all of his life."

Silence. Then the sound of weeping. Finally he said, "I can't talk." It was a memorable moment, this verbal meeting of two Christians, strangers united through tragedy, spiritually, physically, and emotionally. We made plans to meet at his home. I couldn't wait!

As I finished reviewing the events of the past week, my plane began its descent into Phoenix. What a contrast to my last trip to Phoenix, when we were about to say good-bye to our dying son. I felt great joy in my loving reunion with Kathy, who was happily remarried and still living in Phoenix. She will always be precious to us; we've agreed to stay in touch. I was determined to keep the promise I had made to my husband that this trip would result in steps forward, not backward, in the grief process.

On October 23, 1986, Dordt College alumni friends living in Phoenix drove me north, from desert to mountains, from warm to cool, from cactus to pine. The ride prepared me for this momentous meeting. God's creation never seemed more exquisite nor his presence more real. We drove on a winding, wooded road, past the Ponderosa Baptist Church (the kidney recipient's parish) and finally arrived. Clutching the red scrapbook, I rang the doorbell. Dr. and Mrs. Woodrow Finger, two lovely, dignified, articulate Christians, greeted us. I did not feel grief, only overwhelming gratitude for God's providence. Through Dr. Finger the spread of the gospel had continued because Jack had died. This was a *miracle* to me and a *reward* to us. This knowledge has been a major factor in our recovery.

"The communion of the saints" took on new meaning for me. It seemed that ten thousand angels filled that home, and I imagined Jack smiling approvingly from heavenly bleachers. Dr. Finger was eager to learn about Jack: his Christian commitment, his gifts and goals, the circumstances of his death, our family, my husband's work. Together we pored over the scrapbook and read Lydia's letter.

He told me about his life and the events leading up to the transplant. His case had appeared hopeless. He had known he was dying, and the opportunities for a transplant had been remote, his name being far from the top of the list of potential recipients. He had made plans to visit his children in California for a last time, leaving the morning of December 9. But on the evening of December 8 he received a call from the transplant center in Phoenix. A young man, injured in a motorcycle accident, had just died. His kidneys appeared to be a perfect match with Dr. Finger's. He was urged to drive to Phoenix immediately. "It's still a miracle," he said.

For five days his life hung in the balance. On the fifth day, the day of Jack's funeral service in Sioux Center, the kidney "took." Today Dr. Finger swims, jogs, plays tennis, and carries on his ministry with vigor. We talked about his ministry, his belief in the infallibility of God's Word, and more. Our conversation and sharing of the Word strengthened us both.

We went to his church, and I snapped a picture of my new friend behind his pulpit, something that seemed important to me before we went our separate ways. We hugged each other and testified to each other and finally said our good-byes. He marveled that I had shed no tears. "Why not?" he asked.

With a flood of tears just beneath the surface, I said, "For two reasons: because 'I can do all things through Christ, who strengthens me,' and because God has given us a beautiful compensation for a profound loss."

To God be the glory! My mission was accomplished, and I was ready to go home. But I would not rest until Dale, too, could meet these special people.

A year later we stopped for a two-hour layover in the Tucson, Arizona, airport. Dr. Finger and his wife, Theda, greeted us with open arms. He was now preaching in a Baptist church near Tucson. We decided to eat dinner together in the airport restaurant. We talked nonstop, and for Dale's sake Dr. Finger reviewed the circumstances leading to his organ transplant. We reflected on God's goodness and providential leading.

The waitress brought our food. "Shall we pray together?" asked Dr. Finger, reaching for our hands. As his fervent prayers rose to the throne of abundant grace, I imagined Jack's face, radiantly beaming. And I seemed to hear him say, "Behold, and see God's unfathomable ways!"

"Who among all these does not know that the hand of the LORD has done this? In his hand is the life of every living thing and the breath of all mankind" (Job 12:9, 10).

39

Joy

I described a lovely student in one of my letters to Jack. "I'm eager for you to meet and teach Joy Gross," I wrote. "She sings beautifully and is spiritually far beyond her years. Her musicality and her strong Christian principles remind me of you. As an additional asset, she resembles Princess Di."

His reply: "Your description of Joy makes me eager to teach at Dordt College."

God's unfolding plan has continued to astonish us. A week after Jack's funeral Joy observed our son Phil sitting alone in a corner of the student union building. He was crying. Love and sympathy for my husband, her choir director, prompted her to comfort Phil. Returning later to his college apartment, he told his roommates, "I met a girl who really has her head on straight." He then discovered she was the same girl who sang operatic arias in the physical education building as she practiced racketball, while Phil listened and bench pressed in an adjoining room. Before this meeting Phil had known Joy only from a distance. Friendship grew into love. When they became engaged Joy solemnly declared, "Mrs. G, I would not be wearing this ring if Jack had not died."

We have witnessed tremendous spiritual growth in Phil, who went on to prepare for the ministry. I recall the postfuneral luncheon when one of the attending ministers probed Phil, "What are you going to do with your life?"

He responded, "I would like to do what my brother was unable to do—make a difference for the kingdom of God."

God's purposes will ripen fast
Unfolding every hour.
The bud may have a bitter taste,
But sweet will be the flower.

William Cowper

The bitter-tasting bud is the loss of Jack. One of the sweet flowers is the gain of our cherished daughter-in-law, Joy.

"Weeping may tarry for the night, but joy comes with the morning" (Ps. 30:5).

40

Time Heals

"TIME heals" is not correct. "Time eases the pain" would be more accurate. Though we are recovering, we will never recover completely. Forward steps are cause for rejoicing. Grievers know they are healing when the following things take place:

1. They begin to care whether they live or die.
2. Their nagging, ulcerlike pain begins to subside.
3. They rediscover the taste of food.
4. They respond to the beauty of the sun, moon, and stars and the rest of God's great creation.
5. Two hours pass without conscious thoughts of the deceased.
6. They can visit the grave and focus on what is (heaven) instead of what could have been (earth).
7. They view life in living color rather than black and white.
8. Laughter is genuine rather than a forced response to humor.
9. They read short articles and remember what they read.
10. They look to the future with increased vitality.
11. They are able to acknowledge the faults of the deceased.
12. The urge to comfort others is stronger than the need to lick their own wounds.
13. Preoccupation with the deceased no longer mars the joy of a family dinner.
14. They can make minor decisions.

15. They can truly rejoice in the accomplishments of their deceased child's contemporaries.
16. Writing a book on the death of their child becomes a possibility.

"The steadfast love of the LORD never ceases, his mercies never come to an end; they are new every morning; great is thy faithfulness" (Lam. 3:22, 23).

41

Baffled

In the lonely winter months following the accident, unanswered questions concerning its details began to plague me. One in particular: Did Jack have any moments of consciousness? I studied the accident report containing the signatures and telephone numbers of two witnesses. I placed the calls with no success, as both people had since moved. I gave up in frustration. It was a closed book, or so I thought.

Going to the "Y" in the nearby city is usually therapeutic and refreshing for Dale. He enjoys the workout, the anonymity, and the break from his heavy schedule.

One afternoon he was joined in the sauna by a middle-aged man who was admittedly stressed. He had lost his parents and a young son in the past year. In addition, he had recently suffered through a divorce. The two men discussed trials and disappointments and conversed for quite some time.

"Have you always lived in this city?" asked Dale.

"No, I moved here from Phoenix a few years ago," revealed the stranger.

"I lost my twenty-seven-year-old son in Phoenix."

"When?"

"In 1983."

"In December?"

"Yes."

"Was he driving a motorcycle?"

"Yes," answered Dale, with cold chills.

"On the corner of Geneva and South Mill?"

"Yes! Yes!"

"I was the first person on the scene of that accident," the man gasped. "I called the police!"

"Oh! Was he conscious? Did he speak?"

"No, he was unconscious and bleeding from the top of his head. I'll never forget his face. I could describe his every feature to you."

Both men were already late for appointments. Both were so upset that when they finally parted they had failed to introduce themselves. We are baffled by God's ways!

"A man's steps are ordered by the LORD; how then can man understand his way?" (Prov. 20:24).

42

Suffering Victoriously

GRIEVERS will testify that as the months go by, suffering victoriously becomes more difficult. We descend into the abyss before we ascend. Pain, frustrations, depression, deprivation, and unending questions continue to surface. How should we as God's children respond to grief?

1. Expectantly. "In the world you have tribulation" (John 16:33). "Count it all joy, my brethren, when you meet various trials" (James 1:2). If God chose the way of suffering for his perfect, only son, how can we his sinful creatures think we will avoid trials and heartaches?
2. Preparedly. How we respond to life's small trials will determine our response to major testings. A faithful and vigorous devotional life is an essential prerequisite to suffering in the will of God.
3. Uncomplainingly. Our willing acceptance of God's sovereign authority in our daily lives will determine our response to adversity. The Israelites grumbling in the wilderness is a negative example. Job's response should be our model: "Shall we receive good at the hand of God, and shall we not receive evil?" (Job 2:10).
4. Patiently. "But if we hope for what we do not see, we wait for it with patience" (Rom. 8:25). God's waiting room is like a classroom, and while sitting there we learn needed lessons and undergo many necessary changes. "Waiting on the Lord" is good

for us. It intensifies our faith, drives us to his Word for comfort, and puts urgency into our daily prayers. We experience the hard way that faith grows in times of suffering. Our patience in waiting will be rewarded, for the things we hope for are as certain as God's promises to us.

5. Obediently. "Although he was a Son, he learned obedience through what he suffered" (Heb. 5:8). This text gives us a modus operandi. It rules out anger, rebellion, clenching our fists at the will of God, and defying God's authority in our lives. Some modern psychologists encourage us to be angry. The Bible does not. *Prolonged* anger is disobedience.

6. Submissively. "My Father, if this cannot pass unless I drink it, thy will be done" (Matt. 26:42). Not only submission but actively willing the will of God is our greatest challenge.

7. Gratefully. "For the Lord disciplines him whom he loves, and chastises every son whom he receives" (Heb. 12:6). Just as earthly parents lovingly discipline their children to teach them needed lessons in obedience, to refine them, to make them more productive, so God deals lovingly with his children. Chastening, unlike punishment, is done in love. Its purpose is teaching and sanctification; the end of the process is eternal life. God is grooming us for eternity. In that light we can say, "Thank you, Lord. You taught us lessons we would not have learned if life had always been a bowl of cherries."

8. Humbly. We bereaved people seem to be at the end of the line when we are engulfed in feelings of hopelessness and helplessness. We search for comfort, but there is no consolation in tangible things. We learn, as did Christian in *Pilgrim's Progress*, to lay our heavy, back-breaking burden

at the foot of the cross. Here, as in no other place, do we find rest and victory. "Come to me, all who labor and are heavy laden, and I will give you rest" (Matt. 11:28).

9. Trustingly. "Though he slay me, yet will I trust in him" (Job 13:15 KJV). Oswald Chambers calls this "the most sublime utterance of faith in all the Bible." Oh, to possess that kind of faith!

10. Confidently. "But he knows the way that I take; when he has tried me, I shall come forth as gold." (Job 23:10). God is accomplishing his purposes. We believe that. Some of the purposes we see; others we do not see and don't need to. We go forward in the confidence that "all things work together for good to them that love God, to them that are called according to his purpose" (Rom. 8:28 KJV). Good? Is this suffering, this unusual loss good? If *good* refers to the presence of our loved ones, our material possessions, our human power, our social prestige, then it is not good. However, *good* does not refer to the external but to the internal—our relationship to Jesus Christ. And when by his power and grace his name is glorified, our faith is greatly enlarged, and we increasingly yearn for our own place in glory, then we testify that these momentary afflictions are good. The God who lovingly and wisely sent us this monumental loss is beautifully sustaining—no, carrying—and delivering us out of this affliction.

43

A New Song

GOD has put a new song in our lives—a darling grand-daughter. Watching her take her first wobbly steps toward the outstretched arms of her adoring daddy reminds me of our progress through grief.

We take baby steps as we walk this road. We fall. We get up again. Over and over. Gradually our steps, by God's power, become steadier. We have our eyes fixed on the open arms of our loving, heavenly Father, meeting him in glory, and hearing him say:

"Well done, good and faithful servant; you have been faithful over a little, I will set you over much; enter into the joy of your master" (Matt. 25:21).

44

Memories

MEMORIES of Jack evoke a variety of feelings; they can raise me to heights or send me to depths. But God forbid that they should gradually fade away! Whether they are of the mundane or the glorious moments in my child's life, whether of his failures or his achievements, it is through those memories that he continues to have an earthly existence, and I cherish them.

We often traveled at night on our cross-country trips, especially when our boys were small. From his bed in the back seat, two-year-old Jack could see the stars twinkling in the sky, a sliver of a moon, and Mom and Dad sitting close in the front seat with mugs of coffee. He was wrapped up in his favorite fuzzy, colorful Indian blanket, feeling warm and secure.

We asked, "What is love, Jack?"

He answered, "Love is like a warm blanket." All was well with his world—and ours.

I remember with great tenderness.

I received a telephone call from Jack's second grade teacher. He was crying in school, finally admitting, "I have too many songs for my piano lesson, and I don't want to discourage [his actual word] my parents." Neither we nor his piano teacher were aware that he was overburdened and that we were pushing too hard. What is the fine line between encouragement and undue pressure on your child who is gifted and seemingly able to absorb like a sponge as much as you give him?

I remember with some regret.

Every weekday began the same way—an early morning rush to get to school on time. This day was no exception for Jack in third grade and Bob in first. We exchanged our kisses, and I asked, "Did you remember to brush your teeth?" I received an emphatic yes from both boys.

They had nearly completed the half-mile walk to school, when Jack was overcome with guilt. "Bob, you know very well that we didn't brush our teeth." Saying no more, he turned around and walked all the way home from school for a fresh start, clean teeth, and clear conscience.

I remember with a warmhearted chuckle.

At age twelve Jack won first place in an interscholastic piano competition. He was asked to perform his contest piece at our school's PTA meeting. I was seated next to the piano, as accompanist for the audience singing. Unfortunately, by this time he was tired of the piece, of practicing, of performing. He did not play well, he had a memory lapse, and he made numerous mistakes. But what he did recall ever after was my whisper in his ear during the polite applause: "Bow, if you dare!"

I remember, laughing at a memory he detested.

The poster in an Evergreen, Colorado, drugstore read: "Performance of Brahms' *Requiem* this evening," stating the time and place. What an unexpected bonus on a summer night after a day of family travel and mountain hiking. Since Dale had just conducted this work with his college choir and symphony orchestra, it was of special interest to us and to our three boys. They listened intently, evidenced by nine-year-old Jack, who accurately commented afterward, "It was good, but the piccolo player made a mistake. He played a B flat instead of a B natural."

When I remember his musical genius, his creative mind, and his pleasant nature, and when I contemplate the contribution he could have made to church, school, and community, my faith is severely challenged.

At age sixteen, Jack was already an accomplished musician. One spring day he came home from high school and announced, "I have decided that I do not want to take any more piano lessons. You always said that my career would be *my* choice."

I countered, "Yes, your career is your decision, but God gave you many unusual talents. If you wish to discontinue your music study when you graduate from high school, you may do so. But for now you must take these gifts and develop them. Period." We were at an impasse. The elaborate turkey dinner I had lovingly prepared was eaten in less-than-loving silence that evening.

Apparently he thought better of his decision, because the next day he returned from school, gave me a pat on the backside (the equivalent of a kiss when a boy is sixteen) and said, "Mom, thanks for standing up to me. A lot of parents are afraid of their kids and back down. I don't really want to quit, and you won't hear me complain about this again." And I didn't. Not long before he died, he recalled this insignificant incident and commented to his wife, "I wish I had not ruined that nice turkey dinner Mom cooked."

I treasure the memory of his sensitive and thoughtful heart.

Dinner table talk could be noisy when our four boys were home, especially since their ages ranged from toddler to college age. Girls were often the topic of discussion, and this evening was no exception. Jack was receiving unsolicited advice from his dad. "Jack, today I had a telephone conversation with the neatest girl from Calgary, Alberta. Her name is Kathy Sanderse. She's an incoming freshman with a high GPA, is musically gifted, and you'd better grab her before someone else does. Now remember that name, because she's going to be your wife." We all laughed heartily, and it was promptly forgotten.

However, that proved to be prophetic. Jack and Kathy met, dated, and loved each other very much, facing the future with a deep faith in God, and enjoying their many common interests. They were married on August 2, 1979, in a beautiful, creative, God-glorifying ceremony, with Jack's beloved grandfather officiating. It was one of the happiest family days we have ever known. We received our first daughter in every sense of the word. Kathy marched down the aisle triumphantly to the sounds of brass music, which Jack had arranged and was played by a group of his college friends. Jack sang "Our Wedding Prayer" to his bride, a song written by his father and mother for their own wedding. Together they sang "The Song of Ruth," ending with "if ought but death part thee and me." They were married only four-and-one-half wonderful years. Life for them had just begun.

When I remember Jack and Kathy, overwhelming sorrow sweeps over me, and I feel a deep sense of loss.

"I thank my God in all my remembrance of you" (Phil. 1:3).

45

Scrapbook

EACH of us has a prized possession that we would instinctively grab in the event of a fire or an approaching tornado. More than once a large red scrapbook titled "The Life and Death of Jack M. Grotenhuis" has been lovingly hidden in our storm cellar. Enclosed are the tangible memories of Jack's life. The thickness of the book represents the fullness of his life.

I discovered on that frigid February day I started sorting through his things that Jack had methodically saved much more than I anticipated. As if he had known what a formidable task it would be to organize all of his treasured mementos, the contents were in perfect chronological order from kindergarten to graduate school. He made the mechanics of putting this volume together very simple. The emotional cost is my most stinging reminiscence.

Included in the scrapbook are photographs and poignant keepsakes:

His birth announcement and baby pictures (How young, happy, naive we were!)
Little boy pictures (Jack, did I hug you enough?)
High school days (No rebellious stage; God knew your life would be brief.)
Blue ribbons for piano competitions (nothing less than "superior")
College years (a full and exciting life with friends, recitals, activities, tours)
Marriage (What joy!)

Father's and Mother's Day cards from age five to
twenty-seven (Thank you for being openhearted and
appreciative, beyond our deserving.) and messages
such as the following:

                                          June 13, 1979
Dear Dad:
   Since I can't get up to Sioux Center in person,
will wish you a Happy Father's Day from Iowa City.
   Seriously, I can't think of a better time to thank
you and Mom for all you've done for me—musically
and in every other way. Especially for forking over
for instrumental lessons and not letting me quit.
   You also ponied up for my Christian school
education and for all the long trips we took. (You
could retire early on all the $ you'd have saved by
sitting home summers!)
   Thanks probably most of all for being good to Mom
and us, and providing the best parental models I've
ever known and seen. You've given Kathy and me a
high standard to shoot for in our married life. You've
also convinced me of a biblical view of a marriage
relationship that really works. (Of course, when it's
based on love for the Lord, it's no surprise really.)
Boy, Dad, you're a tough act to follow! Happy
Father's Day again!

                                          Love, Jack

Family travels (Mountains—your passion—beaches,
   desert, canoe trips, Disneyworld, national parks,
   white-water rafting—so many fantastic experiences
   were packed into your twenty-seven years!)
Obituary (Why didn't we voice our objections to your
   motorcycle?)

Also in the scrapbook are his letters home. Excerpts:

114

1980. Grampa's complaint about not "preaching the text" applies more strongly today than it ever did, I'm sure of it. Still think that if I flunk out in music teaching, I'd like to become a preacher. People need a lot more than they're getting from the pulpit nowadays. So much of it is strictly horizontally directed, what God has to say *to man,* and how *we* can apply the message to *our* lives. What in the world is wrong with simply trying to find out what he says *about himself* first of all?

November 1980. At the age of 27, I'd have my doctorate, Kathy would have her B. A. in music, we'd have our schooling over with, and be ready to settle down somewhere. Hopefully a [teaching job] would open up by then and we could have kids. Of course this is all the Lord willing, and it goes without saying that a terrible lot can happen in the next two or three years. We could be dead by then.

January 1981. Well, it looks as though I am going to have to eat my words. I told you once not too long ago that I didn't believe Dad would hit the big time until he got his profile on the cover of a Jensen publication. Well, lo and behold, if he isn't on the front cover of "May the Road Rise Up to Meet You." . . . By the way, whether it was because I was thinking more about you last night because of the Jensen music or not I don't know, but I had a nightmare last night that someone came and told us that Dad had died, and it seemed so real, was just awful. Blecchh.

October 25, 1981. Well, if this is any consolation, if a truck runs over me tomorrow, at least you know we're doing well and life has been good for us.

It's no secret that whenever I think of what I should choose for electives, it's always with a view to what the Dordt music department would need. It's probably dumb to think about that, but I do anyway. So if Dad has any brilliant ideas on what they're going to need in their next teacher, let me know. I still think with the background you gave me in piano and instruments, with Dordt's educating me, and with going back to grad school and getting more background in whatever they might need in the future, plus with the experiences I've gone thru in the last two years, I'd be more qualified than anybody [they might consider for a position] as far as broad background goes. But I'd be really interested to know what Dad thinks Dordt could use in their next music teacher so I can get a jump on the position, if it ever opens up. But I first have to pass grad school, and two or three years is a ways off yet, so we'll wait and see first if I get the sheepskin, and leave the rest to God.

May 10, 1981. We heard a good sermon this morning on giving . . . we still don't tithe as a whole church. . . . We talked about that for a while and decided that perhaps all the good things that have happened to us in the past weeks are because we have been very faithful in our giving. We tithe from everything including my choir money, Kathy's money, our mileage money, etc. Not that it stops there, of course. But I figure, how can you possibly expect the Lord to bless you when you scrimp in what you give him from your paychecks.

June 20, 1982 (Phoenix). About time to eat. Roast, potatoes, bean salad, YUM. Can't complain about anything on this end. I still can't figure out why we've been so blessed. I always figured our good year in

Iowa City was God's way of giving us a little rest after two years of teaching, but can't use that excuse anymore. We simply have to give thanks for it all, and be good stewards of our time, talents.

March 17, 1983. We've had spring break this whole week. I worked on a Beethoven analysis assignment, practiced voice, and then yesterday took the ultimate trek: I rode my motorbike up to Four Peaks. It's over 110 miles round trip, and 40 of those miles are on the worst road imaginable, filled with ruts, semiwashouts, little streams going right over the road (spring runoff) and so steep in places that I was riding 10 mph in first gear for two miles at a time. Hiked for two hours on a trail that took me thru pine trees, across little creeks, overlooking views of the valley and of Roosevelt Reservoir. Just fantastic. Ate my lunch up there, then started back. Took a different trail on the way back and ended up bushwacking for a half hour till I found the original trail. Saw other bikers up there on true trail bikes, and bragged to myself that I'd done it (over 4,000 foot climb in 20 miles) with a "domestic" little overgrown moped. The ride down off the mountain was hairy; I wiped out twice, skinned my hand once, and racked up my knee with a hole in my jeans. One of my blinkers is dangling from a wire, but it was bent anyway from a previous wipeout. So finally got it all out of my system. After the ultimate test, there are no more "mountains to climb." Good thing!

March 4, 1983. I hope you two never move here to live like some of these snowbirds do; I'd be ashamed of you if you did, living here in the winter like some of the people who do nothing but golf, or as one guy I see every day who lives in the apartment complex—just stands by his nice big white car and watches the cars and people go by, as if he has nothing better to do, which he probably doesn't. Frankly, if that is what's in store for me, I'd just as soon die before I reach retirement age.

In Jack's demanding master's and doctoral programs he had maintained a perfect grade-point average. Someone asked me if I felt that all of Jack's years of training were a "waste." I replied, "Absolutely not; he is using every bit of that preparation for service in heaven." I believe that with all of my heart. Besides, he had goals and work that satisfied him; more important, he lastingly enriched the lives of numerous people he touched, as seen in the following letters:

Jack Grotenhuis is an administrator's dream. He is steady, versatile, talented, personable, conscientious, and knowledgeable. His instrumental and keyboard skills add a valuable dimension to his choral and vocal emphasis. To complement all of these fortunate factors he is married to a lovely and talented woman. I recommend Jack Grotenhuis without equivocation (from the University of Iowa).

Jack is a unique candidate for many different combinations of collegiate musical responsibilities . . . .
Jack Grotenhuis is a rare combination of excellences and I am happy to recommend him . . . .
Jack Grotenhuis is one of the most outstanding doctoral students with whom I have worked . . . (from Arizona State University).

I value these university recommendations; I am grateful for what Jack was and the efforts he put forth with the gifts God gave him. But what I treasure most is the reference from his professor-father, at Dordt College: "In conclusion, may I add that Jack is every father's dream of a son."

The completed scrapbook was well worth the hours of hurtful effort. I felt a sense of accomplishment—that of putting many of the facets of Jack's life and death "under one cover." I would encourage any grieving parent to risk the pain to produce such a finished, treasured product.

46

Letters

FINALLY, important among my keepsakes of Jack are the many letters we received after his death. Two I especially cherish are the following, the first from a college friend of his and the second from an Arizona State University student.

The death of one so young and talented is always a tragic event—but the death of our dear friend Jack is as "un-tragic" as such a catastrophe can possibly be. So many people—even believers—search for shreds of assurance in their loved one's life and words. But no search is necessary, for Jack's entire life—down to the most mundane details of his day-to-day existence—was a marvelous testimony. We can all share in the comfort of the resurrection. No one who knew Jack could argue with his conviction; I thought Bob [brother] put it very well: "Jack was twenty years ahead of the rest of us in sanctification." Although we can't know for sure, his life surely seemed to indicate a "head start," a testimony to the realness of God's providence. Jack had such an unswerving conviction in his life, and his twenty-seven years were certainly used for the glory and honor of our Lord.

There are people God sends into your life who always make your life and your experience better. Jack was such a person. We were fellow students at

ASU. He sang in my doctoral recital, sat next to me in many classes, and was one of my closest friends. We always knew Jack was special, not only for his talent (he was second to none in this regard), his unpretentious manner (he was so easy to talk to), but also for his consistent walk with God. Jack and I had many talks about spiritual things. Jack was a true Christian. Somehow I know you know this because you must have been a real influence in his life. He always spoke well of you.

Jack's influence on my life has made a difference. He is missed, deeply, but we both know he is singing in perfect harmony in heaven.

I am reminded of the scripture in Psalm 90:12 NIV: "Teach us to number our days aright, that we may gain [present] a heart of wisdom."

If the purpose of this life is to "gain a heart of wisdom" that we might present it to God on our home-going, then Jack was ready to go.

Jack's influence on the students and professors at ASU, I know, will be of comfort to you. Because of Jack's coming to ASU we are all a little richer, and because of Jack's going we are all diminished.

May God continue to comfort you as only he can.

47

Conclusion

Jack was, I believe, an unusual, outstanding young man. His legacy to his family, friends, and associates is now our comfort. Every person is unique and valuable to his or her family and to the Lord. Ultimately, every Christian parent who loses a child cherishes the value of that child's life on earth and life in heaven. Finally, there comes an acceptance of what was and what was not to be, and an acceptance of what no longer is. But greatest of all is the joy over what there now is for the child who has died in the Lord.

I end with an excerpt from a paper Jack wrote for his English 200 class, May 2, 1975, which he titled "The Theme of Death in the Light of Scripture." My prayer is that he speaks for all Christian children who have died.

From the stories we've read so far, it appears that each of the characters had peace within themselves before they died. It's a pity though, that these people, though dying in peace, missed the mark as far as *dying in the Lord is concerned*. In each of their cases, the individual finally reconciled himself to the fact that he or she was going to die, and it appears to me that they somehow found the strength *within themselves* to be calm and accept death.

The believer however, should realize how humanistic this approach to death is. The story characters may even believe they will have an afterlife, but there is no salvation apart from Christ. No mention is made of Christ, or any mediator or atoning work for that matter. We as Christians need not be fearful of death, for the Bible is full of comfort for those who die in the Lord.

Psalm 116:15 NIV says: "Precious in the sight of the LORD is the death of his saints." Proverbs 14:32 KJV says: "The righteous hath hope in his death." We are taught to live in humility before God while we are on this earth and should pray that the Lord will "teach us to number our days" (Ps. 90:12 NIV).

The biggest comfort for the Christian in time of death is that his death is not meaningless. The characters in our story really had little to live for; they may have thought they did, but actually they were dying without salvation. I didn't read of any repentance of sins (though the Christian knows that once he is saved, it is for eternity). It would be fine if we knew beforehand that the dying person had been a Christian, but I don't read that, and that's why I hesitate to believe that anyone who feels this superficial peace of mind and heart can die in the Lord. We as Christians can only rejoice with Paul when he says, "Whether we live, we live unto the Lord; and whether we die, we die unto the Lord; whether we live therefore, or die, we are the Lord's" (Rom. 14:8 KJV).

Song of Triumph

Dale Grotenhuis
1984

Revelation 15:3–4

Great and marvelous, marvelous are your deeds,
    Lord God Almighty.
Just and true are all your ways;
You, O Lord, over all are King.
Who will not fear you, O Lord,
    and bring great glory to your Name?

For you alone are holy.
    Alleluia, alleluia, alleluia.
You alone are holy, are holy.
    Alleluia, alleluia, alleluia.

All nations shall come and worship before you,
For your mighty and holy acts have been revealed.
Great and marvelous are your deeds,
    Lord God Almighty.

Bob, Phil and Joy, and Tom

you ministered to me in unique ways
during the writing of our family's journey through grief.

I treasure your perception
as you provided
in just the right doses
at just the right time
stimulation, support, and love.

I thank God for each of you!